Rocklands

Rocklands

On Becoming the First Generation of Black Psychologists
in Post-Apartheid South Africa

Liezille Jean Jacobs

AFRICAN
MINDS

I read the manuscript four times, and I was triggered, troubled, traumatised and totally impressed by this scholarly work which Prof. Liezille Jacobs has written using psychobiography to take the reader on her journey as a young black girl from Rocklands in Mitchell's Plain to being the first black woman heading the Psychology Department at Rhodes University.

She had to deal with being assaulted by an uncle when she was ten years old, to being bullied and harassed by boys and girls at school, to dealing with her political activist father who is her hero but who was also a patriarch, abusive and suffered from alcohol use disorder. In addition, an abusive husband and various bullies and patriarchs in academia contributed to her struggling with low self-esteem and imposter syndrome. She depicts her mother as having very little agency in relation to her husband; however, she is also responsible for motivating her daughter to succeed. Foucault's notion that we all have power comes to mind.

She uses these challenges as opportunities for self-development and supporting others. Her strategies will assist others to cope in the corridors of academia.

I am not aware of any other South African scholarly work which recognises how a country's political climate impacts individual, families, communities and then inserts the personal and, dare I say, the intimate, to produce an academic text of this stature.

It is an academic book which I hope will serve as a "go to read" for all black women starting their careers as academics, and indeed all academics. This book is for the patriarchs in families and especially in academia. You know who you are. It is a book I wish I had read decades ago, and which I will recommend to all who I mentor and to other mentors and, in fact, to all academics.

– Prof. Cheryl Potgieter, Director: Gender, Justice, Health and Human Development Research and Doctoral Leadership Academy, Durban University of Technology

When I first read the manuscript, I was excited and disturbed in equal measure. Excited because here was a break with conventional style and method when it comes to writing serious academic texts. The academic language was direct and unpretentious. The narrative thread that carried the story was nevertheless clear and consistent. Some of the elements of a solid psychobiography were evident throughout. This was exceptional academic writing that would no doubt upset the orderly, positive applecart that characterises much of academic psychology. Good, I thought. Disturbed because of the acutely painful stories being told about what a young, black girl, a student, mother, researcher, teacher and assistant had to live through in the long and treacherous road to becoming a critical psychologist and, more recently, the first black woman as head of the psychology department at Rhodes University.

– *Prof. Jonathan Jansen, Stellenbosch University*

Successfully fusing several narratives, including narratives of the travails faced by black women in academia and the harshness of life in communities inhabited by those relegated to the margins of society, with *Rocklands*, Liezille Jacobs offers us a courageous and captivating read. This book is both inspired and inspiring.

– *Prof. Norman Duncan, University of Pretoria*

Published in 2024 by African Minds
4 Eccleston Place, Somerset West, 7130, Cape Town, South Africa
info@africanminds.org.za | www.africanminds.org.za

The views expressed in this publication are those of the author.
When quoting from any of the chapters, readers are requested to acknowledge the author.

ISBN (paper): 978-1-928502-89-0
eBook edition: 978-1-928502-90-6
ePub edition: 978-1-928502-91-3

Copies of this book are available for free download at: www.africanminds.org.za

ORDERS:
African Minds
Email: info@africanminds.org.za

To order printed books from outside Africa, please contact:
African Books Collective
PO Box 721, Oxford OX1 9EN, UK
Email: orders@africanbookscollective.com

Contents

Foreword by Jonathan D. Jansen ix
Preface xii

Chapter 1: Introduction 1

PART ONE

Chapter 2: Rocky times in Rocklands 15

Chapter 3: Displacement and the worst day of my life 25

Chapter 4: Bad times in Breidbach 30

Chapter 5: Living in two dimensions 40

Chapter 6: A university orientation 45

Chapter 7: Flashbacks and a "new" father 50

Chapter 8: The liberation struggle continues 59

Chapter 9: Love and marriage 65

Chapter 10: Becoming a doctor 72

Chapter 11: Four times a postdoc 79

Chapter 12: Psychology's unfinished business 95

Chapter 13: 1 in 9 107

Chapter 14: Future Professors Fellow 112

PART TWO

Jacobs on autopsychobiography 119

 Theory 121
 Research questions 124
 Methods 124

Conclusion 139

References 141
About the author 149

Foreword

Since Chabani Manganyi's award-winning book, *Apartheid and the Making of a Black Psychologist*, there has been a major lacuna in the social sciences generally, and in psychology in particular, about the biographies of scholars who lived their professional lives on both sides of the 1990s. The decade that marked South Africa's transition to democratic rule. Liezille Jacobs' first scholarly book fills that gap, and it is a stunning contribution to our understanding of how disciplinary lives are led inside the turmoil of institutions and our still unsettled democratic transition.

When I first read the manuscript, I was excited and disturbed in equal measure. Excited because here was a break with conventional style and method in writing serious academic texts. The academic language was direct and unpretentious. The narrative thread that carried the story was clear and consistent. Some of the elements of a solid psychobiography were evident throughout. This was exceptional academic writing that would no doubt upset the orderly, positive applecart that characterises much of academic psychology. Good, I thought.

Disturbed because of the acutely painful stories being told about what a young, black girl, a student, mother, researcher, teacher and assistant had to live through in the long and treacherous road to becoming a critical psychologist and, more recently, the first black woman head of the psychology department at Rhodes University. Nobody should have to navigate such a hard and unforgiving road to becoming a scholar and yet this is the reality of what it took for the author to rise in her profession, despite the formidable obstacles faced in the family, on the Flats, on campus, and in the halls of the academy.

There are some prominent books and other publications that have appeared in recent times on the lives of black and women students in South Africa's universities. The #MustFall moment certainly brought the harshness and hardships of student experiences to the forefront of national consciousness. There is, by way of contrast, a dearth of literature on the challenging lives of academics in higher education institutions and, in particular, of those trying to build an academic identity for themselves.

An enormous composure and discipline is required to put together such storied experiences inside the cover of a book that will be accessible enough for anyone to read. I know that the author struggled for months with that often-invisible tussle of conscience that authors grapple with in the dead of night. What to leave out? Should you talk about a rapist in the family? What would the family think of me? Is it ethical to mention by name the senior academic head who systematically broke you down? What about lawyers and the Protection of Personal Informaton Act (POPIA)? Do you speak about racist white students who questioned your credentials and undermined your authority as a young lecturer? Would such written revelation be read as weakness or, worse, revenge? Surely a positive book that inspires and glosses over personal and private pain would make more of an impression?

Like any other author, Liezille Jacobs struggled with these questions. The need to tell the truth must obviously be balanced against the legal and personal consequences of revelation. I believe this book gets the balance right and, in the process, offers the broader public and university people a disturbing window through which to observe the operations of broken community as well as the academic environment.

There is, of course, a place for restraint in academic writing. Manganyi achieves this well through his surgical account of the workings of racism at places like Wits University and academic hospitals en route to becoming a black psychologist. But I felt it was almost unethical to ask for such restraint in the case of this book because of the harsh and, dare I say, still existing practices that undermine young academics trying to break through in their careers; practices such as bullying, neglect, discrimination and betrayal.

Not all of academia is like that. I would like to believe that there are many more mentors and coaches in the academy today than in past decades, largely because of a growing institutional awareness of the mental and emotional health needs of both students and academics. And yet it would be naïve to believe that every department is a safe space for aspirant academics or that every laboratory offers junior staff equal and affirming opportunities for growth and development.

That is why this book had to be written and why it should be essential reading for any young scholar wanting to avoid the pitfalls of university life but also snap up the opportunities that present themselves along the journey of becoming a psychologist or chemist or engineer or, most of all, a good academic citizen.

To this end, this intriguing new book will help generations of current and future scholars to map their own paths towards what still is one of the most exciting jobs on the market: a university academic.

Jonathan D. Jansen
Distinguished Professor of Education
Stellenbosch University

Preface

*I have a dream that our story gets published and then maybe
one day we all will get some justice* – Juice Brown

At times it felt like I had my heart in my mouth when I was writing
about my personal life and my lived experience in becoming a critical
psychologist in post-apartheid South Africa. Many of us have lived
long enough to have a few chapters we wish we could erase. No doubt
you have a few stories you wish you could rewrite. We all do. We call it
regret. Yet, chances are the decisions that lead to my greatest regrets
could have been avoided if I had paused to ask myself: "What story
do I want to tell?"

For the most part, as a black-bodied woman, my story is about
showing up for an invisible war. I expect to be discredited. I expect
my experiences to be dismissed. Sometimes it is disconcerting, but
it also proves the power that I must garner to put the oppressor on
edge. Inspired by Bantu Steve Biko's *I write what I like* (1981), dare I
say, writing this book has felt like slave chains and ankle cuffs being
released as each chapter unfolded.

This book is important, not only for what it tells but for what
it expects of you. If you are a white feminist, this book may make
you uncomfortable. But I hope that you will take a step back, be

accountable for the role you play in racial and gender discrimination instead of using tears to avoid it. If you are a black woman, and/or queer, I hope my experiences will make you feel seen. If you are a man, read this book for your own education and perhaps liberation.

In my experience, an invisible war is a shameful secret that the oppressor intimidatingly forces the victim to conceal or else face grave consequences. It is invisible because it is a transgression done in secret, with few or no witnesses. It is a war because it is a state of physical and psychological armed conflict. The oppressor inflicts harm to make someone (like me) feel less confident, hopeless and afraid. This kind of violence is what social psychology refers to as a psychological attack.

In no way is this book about an angry black African feminist, battle-bruised and out for revenge. My success is not revenge. This book is about me being a tenacious survivor. But black women are not merely surviving. When we mature and gain insight into the elusive invisible war, we move one step ahead of the oppressor. Especially when *we* expose the oppressors' designs to elicit self-doubt and reactivity from us with phrases such as:

> *You're crazy.*
> *Don't be so sensitive.*
> *Don't be paranoid.*
> *I was just joking. It's all in your mind.*
> *It doesn't mean anything.*
> *You're imagining things.*
> *You're overreacting.*
> *Don't get so worked up.*
> *That never happened.*
> *There's no pattern.*
> *It wouldn't be any different anywhere else.*
> *You're just acting out.*
> *I'm worried; I think you're not well.*

This is a book in two parts. Part One is about becoming, and Part Two is about using what I have become to guide others.

The opening chapters of Part One are the chronicles of the hard-hitting, disturbing and emotionally affecting experiences I faced as a black-bodied girl. My mother says that as a child, I invariably followed all the rules. In retrospect I know that was because I did not want to draw attention to myself. As a child and as a teenager, I was re-traumatised and faced chronic post-traumatic stress. I withdrew socially. My behaviour was what psychologists would refer to as "socially anxious". I had an intense fear of being watched, judged by others and being embarrassed. What led to my social anxiety will unfold in the early chapters of this book. This includes stories about how my family ended up in Rocklands, Mitchell's Plain, created by the apartheid government in the early 1970s as a coloured[1] residence for low- to middle-income families.

The significance of this section lies in how in the midst of tear gas and intimidating Casspir armoured vehicles roaming our streets, I won an essay prize depicting my father's activist role at Rocklands Primary School. I was a straight-A student. I was resilient. I had an absent father because he was a construction worker who could not find work in Cape Town. My mother ingrained it in me that education would free me from poverty and that picture forever lives in my subconscious mind. In 1986 my father met an American who invested in him and he was able to start his own construction company in the 1980s which is why our family moved to the Eastern Cape province of South Africa. We moved back to Cape Town before I matriculated because my father wanted me to study at the University of the Left, the infamous, University of the Western Cape (UWC).

---

1   During the apartheid years (1948–1993), all South Africans were classified in accordance with the Population Registration Act of 1950 into "racial groups" namely, "Black/African" (people mainly of African descent), "Coloured" (people of mixed or Khoisan descent), "White" (people mainly of European descent), or "Indian" (people mainly of South-Asian descent). The provision of services occurred along these "racially" segregated lines. The disproportionate provision of services to different "race groups" led to inequities. State institutions still collect citizen information along these "racial" divisions. In no way do I subscribe to these "racial classifications".

When I registered at UWC in 1995, I was quickly made aware of how much pressure was on my generation as the first "free" psychologists.

I also unravel the transition from girlhood to becoming a woman. I wish I could say that it was a smooth transition but, as we all know, puberty unleashes identity confusion and a conflict between intimacy and isolation. Honestly, we are all a mess during this stage of our lives. However, add bullying, alcohol abuse disorder, apartheid, violence and poverty to the vulnerability of growing pains and it is no wonder that I had social anxiety. It was only later, when I studied psychology, that all my childhood experiences made some kind of sense. Back then, when I would speak out about being bullied, I was shamed and told I needed to stop imagining things. Yet, as I grew older, as a young adult, I found the antidote to unveiling the invisible wars. One battle at a time. How I did this is fully described in the latter half of Part One, the part of this book where I focus on my work-life. As an academic within the field of psychology, I dig deep into the socio-political roots of psychology in South Africa and the question of why I identify as an African feminist and a Christian. These often-opposing doctrines are rarely used in the same sentence. No doubt, there is a constant struggle in my mind. Most Christians I know shy away from feminism, sexuality and issues of race. The black women Afro feminists I know view religion as synonymous with patriarchal beliefs. As far as I am concerned, in his teachings, Jesus demonstrates an early form of feminism. And so has my mom, a retired "housewife" who only found freedom when all her children were grown up. Institutionalised cages of what it means to be woman, an African feminist and a Christian motivate me to deconstruct expressions of patriarchal power in this book.

My story is inspired by Sisonke Msimang's *Always Another Country* and by Desiree Lewis and Gabeba Baderoon's *Surfacing: On Being Black and Feminist in South Africa*. I admire the way in which these African feminists contextualise, to some extent, what I experience as a black, female critical psychologist working in academia. On 23 March 2021, I was about to board a flight from Cape Town to Port

Elizabeth when I walked past a bookstore and was drawn in by a book titled *Reflecting Rogue: Inside the Mind of a Feminist*. I read the entire book on the plane and could not stop thinking about it on the tiring drive home to Makhanda. I read *Rape: A South African Nightmare* a year ago, also on a plane; this time from Durban to Johannesburg. To be clear, I don't only read on planes: I'm a librocubicularist. I love reading in bed. The author of both books, Pumla Dineo Gqola, is my imaginary best friend. We have so much in common. Reading Gqola's writing has inspired me to tell my truth.

As I read the distinguished professor's reflections on what an African feminist is, I re-imagined my childhood. I grew up with a macho patriarch who expected my mother to stay at home, cook, clean and mind the children. Yet, through my adult eyes, I see how my mother – who dropped out of school when she was in grade seven – has been a "closet" feminist all along. As a mother of three myself now, I view my mom's support for my freedom as a force, like a fire burning with desire for me to *get out*. As a child, I did not know what she meant by getting educated to *be free*.

Ava DuVernay's documentary feature, *13th,* and Jordan Peele's feature film, *Get Out*, come to mind when I re-imagine my mother's persistence as a fire metaphor. DuVernay's documentary is a powerful exploration of the African American experience with the US criminal justice system, particularly as it relates to the US Constitution's Thirteenth Amendment and the prison industrial complex (Lopez-Littleton & Woodley, 2018). Through its innovative narrative strategy, the film, distributed on Netflix, challenges traditional film representations of American prisons and instructs the American public on the intersections of race and the criminal justice system (Festa, 2022). It serves as a counter-narrative to the dominant white majority's representations of (imprisoned) African Americans, aligning with the broader context of black resistance and dissent. Jordan Peele's *Get Out* manages a similar feat by exploring the state of race relations in contemporary America through the lens of sci-fi horror (Garrett, 2020).

The more I studied the more entrapped and entangled I became in what it meant to become a psychologist in post-apartheid South Africa. Figuratively, my voice was muddled with philosophical strategies of freedom. My life now, interwoven within the struggles of the institutional cages in post-apartheid higher education, plagued with inequalities, highlights the need to interrogate the discipline of psychology. The stories I tell in latter chapters of this book closely relate to the contention in psychology in Africa, but more specifically the unfinished business of psychology in South Africa. My deeply personal accounts are of the horrific suffering of systemic injustice at academic institutions that perpetuate and cover up the existence of black female bodies' physical and emotional scars with profoundly personal and social consequences.

The first part of the book ends with my interpretation of the complexities within the discipline in post-apartheid South Africa and my journey as an academic within the discipline of psychology. The second part of the book focuses on the method of autopsychobiography and how the data (my biography) are viewed through a psychological lens. I share some of the tools with which psychology, specifically social psychology and critical psychology, provided me to defend my psyche and to identify a psychologically violent threat so that I am always one step ahead of the oppressor.

I often refer to my career trajectory as the road less travelled because I have a melting-pot of experience which is unique and not confined to the career trajectories of the typical psychologist in South Africa. Most academics in psychology are registered within the professional categories of research, counselling, clinical or educational psychology. Even though I have a doctorate in Psychology, I did not opt for a professional master's degree but completed a master's by thesis. I therefore identify as an academic within the discipline of critical and social psychology. In some ways I am self-taught. I did not choose this less travelled path. It chose me. That may sound a bit clichéd, but I remember vividly, not being taught in undergrad or Honours how to work with a qualitative or quantitative research statistical package, post-1994. More about the inequalities in higher education in later chapters.

My purpose is to teach psychology students to think outside of the proverbial box about what it means to be a psychologist in post-apartheid South Africa. Becoming a psychologist should not be confined to sitting in an ivory tower, listening to privileged people's problems, but rather to being a focal part of the social change in communities that are under-resourced. Most students of psychology only find out about the way in which the psychology patient navigates through the mental health system in their clinical or counselling master's internship. Research on this topic illustrates that this is hopelessly too late, and students are burdened with either dropping out or choosing academia as a default rather than practice (Booysen & Naidoo, 2016; Haine & Booysen, 2020). It is with this knowledge in mind that I created the curriculum for critical health psychology at third-year level (which is an exit course). The main theme of this course is to amplify my students' understanding of how the mentally ill client navigates through the public mental health system. I discuss how my experiences within the field of public mental health prepared me to teach a course of this nature.

In 1995, when I was 18, I registered as a first-year student to become one of the Republic's first free psychologists. Then, I had no idea that psychology in post-apartheid South Africa had to address its credibility characterised by Verwoerd's (a white psychologist and architect of apartheid) social injustice within the professional landscape. A multitude of research conducted on the transition of the profession in post-apartheid South Africa suggests that this discipline still trains psychology students as if this is little Euro-America and their clients are lily-white elitists. Corridor conversations with colleagues cement the calamity professional psychology is wrestling with in an ethnographically diverse country. The discipline of psychology in South African higher education is constantly transforming in an attempt to acclimatise to the country's mental health needs, but it falls short because there's a lack of understanding on how to address ongoing debates such as: the benefits/pitfalls of becoming an academic versus a professional psychologist; how dependent professionals in practice are on academics who train future psychologists and how often dialogue is needed to attend to these disputes; how the hierarchical structure of academic versus professional psychologist differs from an interwoven life of struggles within the institutional cages of post-apartheid higher education, and how these debates address systemic historical social inequality stemming from apartheid's unequal division of resources to make sure that all universities are created equal.

These ongoing debates are what I build up to from one section to the next in this book. I do this to shift the focus to the importance of academics within the discipline of psychology; how my upbringing shaped my contribution to the discipline in post-apartheid South Africa because not a lot is known about taking the academic versus professional route in psychology. Herein lies the significance of this book: post-apartheid psychology's active engagement in ongoing and reflexive self-examination to ensure that psychologists are more accessible and truly serve the nation pre-empts the challenge not only for psychology in South Africa, but the entire African continent, if not the world.

I exclude in this book the periods when I needed a break from the life of struggle within the institutional cages of post-apartheid academia and worked as a radio journalist, a TV journalist and a project manager in the fields of tourism and health in non-governmental organisations. These were challenging and very memorable times, however. What I learned from these periods was how much I was drawn to the academic project: that is, finishing my doctoral studies and publishing my research.

I wrote this book with the following people in mind: my parents, my siblings, extended family, friends, colleagues, acquaintances, and my students.

This book is written for everyone who is interested in: the academic project, the factors that influence apartheid's aftermath, the struggles that women, especially black people, experience (in and outside of academia), future psychologists, academic and professional psychologists. In this book I write about how I became, against all odds, a champion of the post-apartheid struggle, a mother, and an academic in the field of critical and social psychology.

1

Introduction

I have nothing to offer except a way of looking at things.
– Erik Erikson

I was born in Cape Town on 24 September 1976 in the Peninsula Maternity Hospital in District Six. This book was inspired by time and place, the layers of complex physical, social, political and cultural systems at play during my personal development. How, amidst the struggles and strife during apartheid, I wanted to make my voice heard in post-apartheid South Africa and reflect on my journey from Rocklands to Rhodes.

I was motivated to write this book in 2019 when Professor Jonathan Jansen interviewed me for his book on the transformative experiences of academics who strive to decolonialise curricula in South African higher education. Professor Jansen only wanted to interview me for a few minutes but once he asked me profoundly thorough questions, I was unable to stop talking and he could not stop gasping at every word. He said that what I had to say needed to be heard, to be read. The fact that my story has not yet been shared publicly concerned him and, after reflection, it troubled me, too.

It is important to note that before I met Professor Jansen, I thought he was an enigma, someone who had the bravery to speak his mind with little consideration of the consequences. His courage and ability to communicate so eloquently on his experiences motivated me to tell my own story.

Upon deep reflection I understood for the first time that becoming a critical psychologist in post-apartheid South Africa was inevitable. My lecturers at the University of the Western Cape's (UWC) psychology department consciously and deliberately prepared me to become a critical psychologist. Here's why. Hussein Abdilahi Bulhan's *Frantz Fanon and the Psychology of Oppression* was a text I would read outside the scope of my training as a psychologist because my lecturers challenged me to think about how South Africa's socio-political climate influenced our psychosocial development (Bulhan, 2004). Critical psychology is psycho-politics, simply put. According to Hook's (2001) understanding of critical psychology, Fanon, a socially conscious psychiatrist, politicises psychology by bringing psychological terms and concepts into the ambit of politics. My autopsychobiography is similar to the analysis in the *Psychology of Oppression* in that it ties my psychological evaluation at each point of my psychosocial development to the socio-political and historical circumstances of post-apartheid South Africa. Critical psychology is synonymous with social justice as this "Redemption Song" lyric adequately frames:

> *Emancipate yourselves from mental slavery*
> *None but ourselves can free our minds*
> – Bob Marley & The Wailers

Convinced that my story would contribute to social change and the growing knowledge of critical psychology in South Africa, I read, again, Professor Chabani Manganyi's memoir, *Apartheid and the Making of a Black Psychologist*. Immediately, I perceived how different our stories were. Manganyi's 2013 essay, "On becoming a psychologist in apartheid South Africa" (an excerpt of his memoir), chronicles some of the barriers and hurdles that he had to overcome to train as a black male psychologist in South Africa when it was unexpected that Africans could train as psychologists.

My experience is different to Manganyi's because I am woman, so our socio-cultural trajectories of becoming psychologists have been different. We differ in age – we come from different eras. Also, our areas of expertise are different. Manganyi's book illustrates his accomplishments as a clinical psychologist, and various leadership positions held in higher education and government. I consider myself to be a critical and social psychologist, which means that our career aspirations differed entirely. Even though we were both trained in psychology.

Unlike Manganyi, my experience is mostly in public mental health research because I spent the greater part of my working life at science councils. Manganyi's book does not focus on his personal life. My account of becoming a critical psychologist in post-apartheid South Africa is deeply personal, although I do give insight into my becoming a critical psychologist from different developmental perspectives. Yet, even in post-apartheid South Africa, I can relate to Manganyi's experiences because I, too, was constantly reminded that I did not deserve my degrees and that I was not good enough to occupy space reserved for whites only. This only served to motivate me to write this book.

You may wonder: "Why write this book and why write it now?" We all have traumas, scars and events that have shaped us positively and, unfortunately, negatively. So many people become victims to their traumatic circumstances, and truly never recover. Others conquer their trauma in powerful ways, sometimes healing their souls or leaving a trail of battered bodies in their wake. My autopsychobiography tells the story of this entire spectrum: no matter who you are, or what you do, if you've ever made an impactful decision and have been struggling to put it behind you, this story is for you. If the world has stepped on you one too many times and you buckled up and said "I've had enough," this is for you. If you've been hurt by someone you once loved, and it was nearly the end of you, this book is for you. Everything that I went through, every part of me that I wished had been kept sacred. Every bit of pain, every small death and all my regrets and failures are all told and represented here. My story's purpose is to show the real-life pain we all have suffered to some degree and the need to heal from it. This is how I became a critical psychologist: part magnet, part mirror of what Wahbie Long, author of "Rethinking 'relevance': South African psychology in context", refers to as *social justice and social change*. I find myself both drawn to (like a magnet) and exposed by (like a mirror) the *discernible association between conditions of social unrest and calls for social relevance* of psychology in post-apartheid South Africa (Long, 2013).

If I could go back in time, before I entered higher education to become a psychologist, before I knew the difference between a professional and applied psychologist, I would have a cup of coffee with the mother of our nation, Winnie Madikizela-Mandela. She and I share the same birthday month. We would probably have celebratory cake with our coffee. I would ask her what she expects women like me to do to improve the state of our country. I would tell her my story but, more importantly, listen to hers. I would ask her what impact someone like me could make in South Africa. I imagine that Winnie Madikizela-Mandela would probably have said that I should go into politics or journalism. But my parents would have overridden such a career choice. I took an aptitude test when I saw a career counsellor in grade 12. My results pointed to a career in psychology.

I am writing this book now because for the past five years, teaching critical health psychology made me aware that most of my psychology students want to study either clinical or counselling psychology. It is time to change that mentality. It is time for the academic project to expose students to different ways of becoming psychologists and/or applied psychologists to make psychology socially relevant and accessible to the disenfranchised. In the words of Derek Hook's *Critical Psychology of the Postcolonial: The Mind of Apartheid*, critical psychology is a perspective – the critical, psychological, and theoretical examination of racism and oppression. South Africa is the chosen contextual backdrop, used to highlight how racism and colonial ideas persist in a post-apartheid world. This is the essence of my philosophical approach as an applied (critical) psychologist.

This book disrupts some of the tenets of a psychobiography (see Kovary, 2011; Manganyi, 2013, 2016; Mathabe, 2018), a research method that explores the lives and personalities of public figures. In this book I use psychological theory to clarify and illuminate historically significant events, processes engulfed by my personal development. Contemporary psychobiography integrates psychoanalytical, personological and narrative perspectives, and has expanded its focus beyond artists to include scientists, politicians, and historical figures. This book is an autopsychobiography because it systematically formulates a life history and interprets it by means of psychological theories (Schultz, 2005).

In my autopsychobiography, I drew inspiration from several bio-graphers and learnt from them the importance of interpreting one's *own* life story in terms of both time and place. According to Schultz and Lawrence (2017, p. 435), psychobiography cannot function in the absence of "rich biographical data". In other words, what I provide in this book is an *auto*psychobiography. This autopsychobiographical approach is adopted to guide the reader, to understand how I interpret my lived experience through a psychological lens. Therefore, I provide a thick description of my biography to date.

In its goal of attempting to understand my upbringing, this book is guided by Urie Bronfenbrenner's (1986) ecological systems theory, specifically my interactions with my environment and society over extended periods of time. According to this theory, an individual exists within layers of social relationships: the household, the family, intimate partners, friendships (microsystems). Interactions among these microsystems, for example, interaction between my community, church, school and work (mesosystem), my interaction/ understanding of a system which I did not have direct access to such as extended family, government, mass media (ecosystem), cultural and societal beliefs, decisions and actions which influenced my development (macrosystems) and changes of my geographical and socio-historical context (chronosystem). To illustrate how Bronfenbrenner's ecological systems theory guides my understanding of my upbringing, I designed a diagram of my personal ecological system below (see Diagram 1).

Bronfenbrenner thought that the society was the factor that influenced children´s development and this is the key to his entire theory. According to Bronfenbrenner's theory on human development, the structure of the society influences everything down to the least detail. Bronfenbrenner's theory (1979) dwells on human development and follows one's growth into a fully competent member of the society. Therefore, it is a developmental psychology theory. This theory is often associated with socialisation which is the process through which human infants begin to acquire the skills necessary to perform as functioning members of their society (see Vygotski's, 2012, socio-cultural theory, Bandura's, 1969, social learning theory and Erikson's, 1966, psychosocial theory, to mention a few).

Bronfenbrenner's (1981) theory is not specifically a theory for education pedagogy, caring or teaching, learning or civilisation or a theory of mental development. Bronfenbrenner's ecological theory is the human development theory. More specifically, Bronfenbrenners's model encompasses the transactional processes between a person's biological and environmental contextual spheres, focusing on changing personal behaviours while accounting for the influences of the social, physical and political environments (Rosa & Tudge, 2013). To place the bioecological theory of human development into a larger context, it is noteworthy to recognise that many of the general perspectives advanced and elaborated on in this theory are also parts of other related lines of theoretical and empirical inquiry into human development. Examples include lifespan psychology and, especially, the work of

Diagram 1: My upbringing according to the ecological systems theory

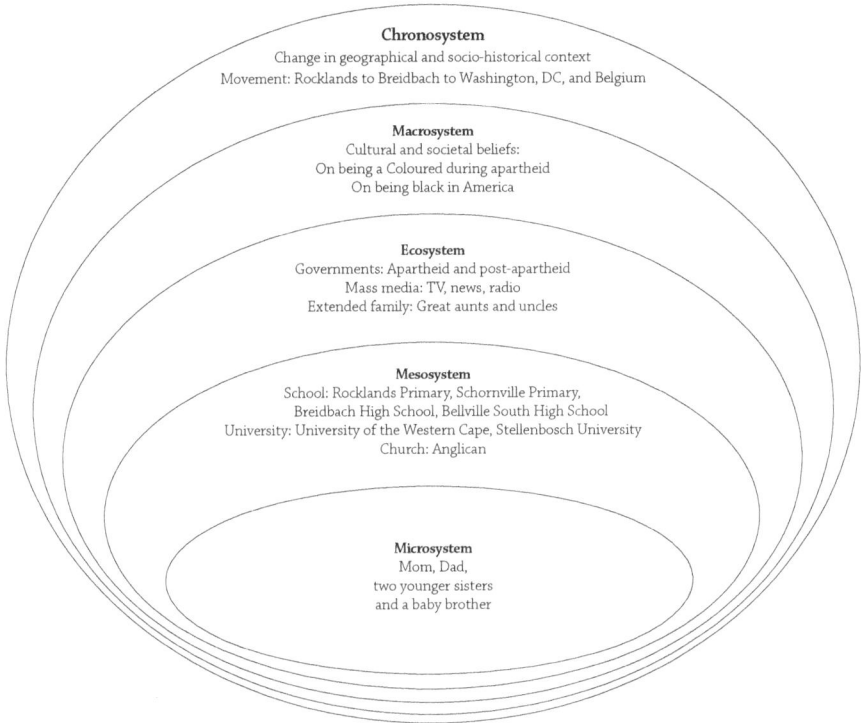

Chronosystem
Change in geographical and socio-historical context
Movement: Rocklands to Breidbach to Washington, DC, and Belgium

Macrosystem
Cultural and societal beliefs:
On being a Coloured during apartheid
On being black in America

Ecosystem
Governments: Apartheid and post-apartheid
Mass media: TV, news, radio
Extended family: Great aunts and uncles

Mesosystem
School: Rocklands Primary, Schornville Primary,
Breidbach High School, Bellville South High School
University: University of the Western Cape, Stellenbosch University
Church: Anglican

Microsystem
Mom, Dad,
two younger sisters
and a baby brother

Robert Cairns (1991), has played a major role in the evolution of the four defining properties of the bioecological model: (1) process, (2) person, (3) context, and (4) time (also known as the PPTC model). Cairns is best known for his pioneering evolution of the bioecological approach of developmental science, in that he contributed to build an interdisciplinary body of work (Bergman et al., 2000; Cairns & Cairns, 2006). The specific profile of the bioecological model of human development, in which the telling of my life story is embedded, is its interdisciplinary and integrative focus on the age periods of childhood and adolescence and its explicit interest in applications to policies and programmes pertinent to enhancing youth and family development (Rosa & Tudge, 2013).

It would be remiss of me to not juxtapose Bronfenbrenner's theory of human development with other mainstream theories of developmental psychology such as Erik Erikson's (1950) psychosocial theory. According to his theory of psychosocial development, successful completion of each stage results in a healthy personality and the acquisition of basic virtues (Erikson, 1966). Basic virtues are characteristic strengths which could be used to resolve subsequent crises (Erikson, 1958b). Failure to successfully complete a stage can result in a reduced ability to complete further stages and therefore an unhealthy personality and sense of self (Erikson, 1963).

Erikson's (1950) approach to the development of the individual is focused essentially on how personality is developed biopsychosocially. His developmental theory contains eight stages, each with a challenge between two polarities (Timm et al., 2022). The stages are trust versus mistrust (0–1 year); autonomy versus shame/doubt (2–3 years); initiative versus guilt (3–6 years); industry versus inferiority (7–12 years); identity versus role diffusion (12–18 years); intimacy versus isolation (20s); generosity versus stagnation (late 20s to 50s); and integrity versus despair (50s and beyond).

Diagram 2: Erikson's psychosocial theory of human development

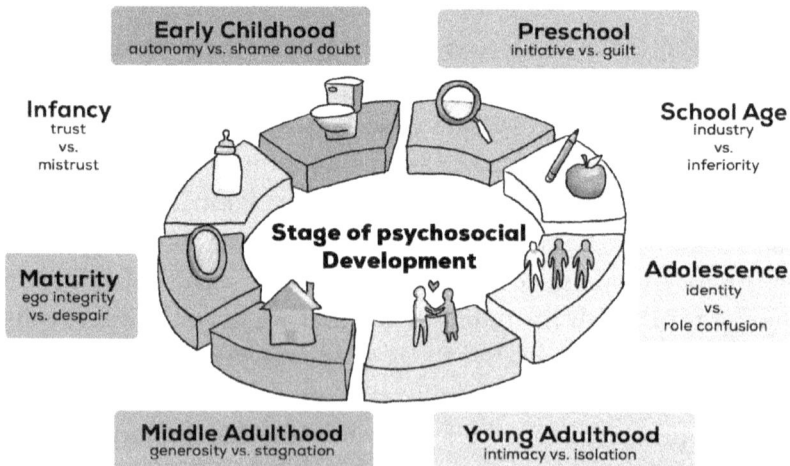

Source: PracticalPsychology

Noteworthy is that Erikson's psychosocial developmental theory is one of many "metaphors for a singular idea" (Cairns, 1991, p. 23). This means that I will attempt throughout the first part of the book to illustrate how lifespan developmental theories such as Erikson's psychosocial theory do not always aid as all-encompassing explanations of my development as an African. This is noteworthy because most South African researchers and academics are working hard to decolonialise our understanding of being in this world (Hook et al., 2002).

I critique Erikson's theory in parts of my own development to prove how my developmental milestones do not necessarily fit neatly into Erikson's framework. My story spans both the apartheid and the post-apartheid eras in South Africa. This autopsychobiography attempts to highlight why *I* became an academic in the field of psychology. Autopsychobiographies are not exclusively about Freudian accounts of how one's childhood led to one becoming a psychologist or having a certain personality type. Autopsychobiography brings attention to one's childhood, adolescence and adulthood. All phases of one's life and the context in which that life unfolds are equally important because an autopsychobiography is not meant to be a diagnosis of pathology – it is not a pathography.

This book has three main aims. The primary aim is to describe and interpret my life through the autopsychobiographical approach embedded in Urie Bronfenbrenner's bioecological approach, with specific emphasis on the interactions of proposed elements of the PPCT model, and appropriate analyses of PPCT which includes both the genetic and environmental spheres of developments (Rosa & Tudge, 2013). Erikson's theory of psychosocial development (Erikson, 1950, 1956, 1958a, 1958b, 1963, 1964, 1965, 1966, 1968) and the incessant teaching of this theory to future psychologists within South Africa mostly without any proviso of specific stipulations, conditions or limitations does not convince me that this Euro-American individualistic stage model fits neatly into the complexities of our South African context. I chose to use this theory to explain my different developmental stages as an illustration of how problematic it is to apply Euro-American, even psychoanalytic, stage models to a people's development without exploration of time and place contexts which are riven with unjust and lingering social economic disparities such as race, class, gender and sexuality. So, I use this theory with contextualised caveats drawing from constructionist perspectives such as Cairns and Dawes' (1996) in "Children: Ethnic and political violence", Nsamenang and Dawes' (1998) "Developmental psychology as political psychology in sub-Saharan Africa: The challenge of Africanisation", and Stevens and Lockhat's (1997) "'Coca-Cola Kids': Reflections on black adolescent identity development in post-apartheid South Africa" amongst other South African developmentalists.

Second, I aim to contribute to the growing academic field of psycho-biography through an *auto*psychobiographical, critical psychology and African feminist lens in the South African context.

Finally, I hope to contribute to the body of knowledge in the scope of critical health psychology in the South African context. Noteworthy, psychobiographers usually contribute to psychological knowledge and the understanding of the development of extraordinary individuals (such as Chabani Manganyi and Neo Mathabe, both extraordinary professors in psychology in South Africa). I would like to change that narrative with my autopsychobiography. I believe that ordinary people like me could reach a broader audience who can identify with the magnitude of the psychological issues that people like me experience. So, this book is about pushing a particular knowledge boundary within the ambit of psychology.

The main characters in this book are people who have influenced my experiences and shaped my career trajectory. My father, a construction worker and freedom fighter, played a huge role in my decision to become a psychologist. He always encouraged me to read and watch the news and acquire general knowledge about South African history to redress past injustices. My mother wanted me to get an education so that I could become an independent woman, unshackled by patriarchy. Last, but not least, my students are the main reason I am motivated to put words to paper that no textbook could ever come close to teaching them because these are my lived experiences. My trials, pitfalls, tribulations and "aha" moments are what I would like to impart to up-and-coming psychologists. Students who, through the impactful experiences I shared with them, have shaped my being-in-this world, are key role players in this academic autopsychobiography.

A precautionary note when reading this book would be that this is a thoroughly personal, graphic account of what I experienced growing up and becoming a critical psychologist in South Africa. My story is grounded in a deep historical context, yet thoroughly of the present black woman's experience in academia.

You have no idea what it takes to live my life. No one writes books about women like me.

The day everything changed. The incest. The shocking day of self-discovery. The divorce. The wrongful death so unfathomable which I still cannot believe that *that* part of me is gone. The break-up. The make-up. The day my friend walked away. The hateful conversation with a Dutch professor. The aftermath of vile remarks made by a male Indian professor now branded on my soul. Those marked moments in time when I gave birth, three times. The hysterectomy. Life before. Life now. The conversation with a rheumatologist that changed my life forever. How is moving on from these gruesome experiences possible? What is the possibility of creating a life that is beautiful again? These are all questions I had when I started writing this autopsychobiography.

In this book I share identity narratives that have enabled me to reflect on who I was, who I no longer am and who I became. Writing an autopsychobiography has been transformative and life changing because it forced me to evaluate my past, present and future in a way that is both profoundly intimate and self-soothing. This book is about how my background (childhood, adolescence and adulthood) led me to become a doctor and professor in psychology. This is my personal account of how my generation (born in 1976, a turbulent year in South African history), became one among the first cohort (registered at university to become a psychologist in 1995) of free psychologists in post-apartheid South Africa.

Critical psychology, as far as I understand it, pivots around one central principle: psychology is and should be politicised to address psychology's unfinished business.

There are some instances of terminology and phrases that could be easily be misunderstood or misinterpreted. Concepts such as psycho-biography, Erikson's psychosocial theory of personality development, black-bodied, woman, critical psychology and African feminist. As a black woman I cannot divorce myself from the inherited scars of my ancestors. Therefore, I identify as an African feminist because there are distinct conditions and margins that the African feminist needs to push. These are all categories that leak into complexities that psychologists problematise. For instance, when people look at me, within seconds, assumptions about my race, gender and class are made based on their perceptions of my cultural-political background. Social psychologists refer to these as "schemata". Through the process of socialisation, gender roles, stereotypes and world views are formed. If you differ from the gender roles (e.g. being an educated woman) society superimposes onto you, you are excluded and othered. Race, however, is a socially constructed imposition and certainly not a biological phenomenon. I have opted to use "black" to include all people who are not white and to indicate how I self-identify. I want this to be as clear as day: my being-in-the-world as a black woman, as an African feminist, is not a matter of pigmentation. Rather, it reflects my mental attitude.

In this book, I identify as a woman, acknowledging the privilege that comes with identifying with the gender roles assigned to me at birth based on my sex. The book acknowledges the struggles faced by a queer individual who identifies with female experiences and honours them. As an African feminist I have to be intersectional in my view of feminism. This means that I am done walking on eggshells.

PART ONE

2

Rocky times in Rocklands

My earliest memory is of when my family lived on the Cape Flats in Rocklands, Mitchell's Plain.

Before I was born, my parents lived in District Six. District Six no longer exists. Yet, mapping the memories, politics, place and identity of District Six, resurrects the community spirit of belonging and nostalgia for belonging (McEachern, 1998). District Six was an urban space in the heart of Cape Town razed by political manipulation (Hart, 1988). Under the apartheid regime's Group Areas Act, District Six was declared a whites-only area. With that, almost all the buildings were bulldozed (Layne, 2008). Further, many residents were forcibly removed from this once mixed-race residential area; a city district which gave people like my parents a sense of place and belonging. My parents were forced to relocate several more times before they "settled down" in Mitchell's Plain.

My story of becoming a critical psychologist in post-apartheid South Africa starts in Rocklands, Mitchell's Plain.

Becoming a part of the Rocklands community was essentially about participating in the freedom movement. But that came with several conditions and there were people who did not belong to our community. Your membership would be revoked if you were an "*impimpi*" (a sell-out), pretending to be part of the freedom movement by attending political meetings and then feeding information to the military. When you were found out for being a sell-out, the punishment was a slow, agonising public death by torture: they would put a tyre around your neck, lace it with petrol and set you alight.

The conditions of membership provided our community with emotional security, collective identity, a unique language, and a strong sense of belonging because, frankly, who would want such a gruesome and disgraceful death?

In Rocklands people rebelled against the government's order for people to speak "*beskaafde*" (proper) Afrikaans. Even today, passed on from one generation to the next, people from Cape Town, and Mitchell's Pain specifically, are known for their distinctive Afrikaans dialect.

Another element that membership in our community fostered was the necessity to connect to the new environment and the people that had been moved there. Membership in Rocklands was like an emotional crutch to a displaced people who were forcibly removed from their homes by the apartheid state.

Membership of the Rocklands community demarcated a protected space from the army but also sell-outs and, later on, the gangs. Membership not only provided us with physical safety (knowing when the armed forces would raid), but with much-needed psychological safety that depended on loyalty and trust. The understanding of psychological safety was first presented by organisational behavioural scientist, Amy Edmondson (1999, p. 351), who coined the phrase and defined it as "a shared belief held by members of a team that the team is safe for interpersonal risk-taking".

Becoming a critical psychologist in post-apartheid South Africa taught me that my people needed unique cultural markers to feel protected against threat and the boundaries that revoked membership. I'm pretty good at blocking out painful memories and my parents tried their best to protect me from traumatic experiences. But growing up during my early years, throughout apartheid, they often fell short, unfortunately. What I have held in for too long are the stories I overheard my parents retelling about their lives in District Six. So, I feel as if I have a profound sense of responsibility to share some of them because there's power in allowing your voice to be heard. And my voice matters.

One day I overheard my parents describe District Six as though it was still there. Suddenly, the heart and soul of Cape Town had moved to the middle of Mitchell's Plain. My parents described District Six as having a rich cultural history and a sense of community that they longed for when they were displaced to Rocklands. I will never forget how much sadness consumed me as I overheard their stories. When I could no longer stand it, I would walk in on their conversation. I will never forget the look of horror in their eyes when I stepped into the room. They immediately changed the topic and the tension in the room was palpable.

Later, as an adult, my father and mother told me how they met as teenagers in Crawford. Crawford was another of the outlying areas that coloured people were forcibly moved to by the apartheid government. Until Crawford was declared a whites-only suburb, and my parents were deported to Mitchell's Plain.

A significant amount of forcible uprooting of people does not take a critical thinker to conclude that such displacements would inevitably cause an uprising.

Becoming a critical psychologist in post-apartheid South Africa shed light on the great sense of loss and displacement my parents felt, and probably are still grappling with to this very day, due to chronic trauma. Critical psychologists believe traditional psychology misses the mark when considering how power differences between social classes and groups can impact the mental and physical well-being of individuals or disenfranchised groups. My need to become a psychologist in post-apartheid South Africa underscores my desire to grasp what social and community psychologists refer to as the deep desire humanity has to connect and be part of a group in order to attain a common social identity and a sense of belonging. The importance of belonging to the Rocklands community breathes life into my family's unique lived experiences.

Historically, unemployment is an intractable problem in Mitchell's Plain. I had an absent father who travelled all over Southern Africa. He was a construction worker who could not find work in Cape Town. His father died when he was young. He sacrificed his own education so that his younger siblings could study. He was a father and an activist.

"Who's in and who's out?" That was basically how my father started and ended every political meeting held in our living room. I think the reason why he said that twice was to reiterate emotional and psychological security, and to protect group intimacy. By asking "Who's in and who's out?" and receiving positive chants like "*A luta continua!*", he created trust and the cadres were more comfortable to share information and strategies.

My father was at Rocklands community hall (now a national heritage site) on 20 August 1983 when the United Democratic Front (UDF) was launched, an important and symbolic event in the freedom movement. The UDF was established as a non-racial structure opposing apartheid. Its slogan read: "UDF unites, apartheid divides" (Seekings, 2000). It positioned the movement at the forefront of the transition from apartheid to a democratic state (Suttner, 2004).

In November 1983, after a referendum approved the government's racially divisive constitutional plans, widespread rent and transport boycotts broke out country-wide (Jacobs, 2010). Our country was on fire. I was eight years old.

At eight years old, according to Erikson's (1958b) psychosocial developmental crisis, I was supposed to have acquired skills deeming me competent by societal standards or I would face an inferiority complex. Given that the government at that time was bent on destroying and restricting our freedom, it is deplorable, to say the least, that a young black girl could have been expected to display any shred of competency. For instance, in 1983, when the UDF was officially launched in my hometown, F. W. de Klerk's wife, when asked about the coloured vote said this: "You know, they are a negative group … a non-person. They are the people that were left after the nations were sorted out. They are the rest" (Maja-Pearce, 1994, p. 135).

Pause. Read that quote again. I heard her say this on the radio. I was scared and confused. I witnessed so much violence and so many protests. Social anxiety influenced my daily life and as a result, I refused to participate in sports at school. I asked my mother to write sick-notes to excuse me from participating in anything that drew a crowd. My experience appears to align with Erikson's identity formation when exploring relationships between the identity, agency, power and cultural worlds of practice (Sneed et al., 2006).

However, my inferiority complex opened a Pandora's box in which tracts of dialogic space sat unexplored; where socio-cultural researchers could consider Erikson's psychosocial theory of development, especially during apartheid (Sneed et al., 2006).

Feminist standpoint theory's analysis of Erikson's theory on lifespan, psychosocial emphasis and the notion of agentic identity development is useful in the post-apartheid multicultural context (Hekman, 1997). Arguably, what agency could I possibly have had when I was eight years old? Black feminist critic bell hooks captures the unique standpoint of what the outsider within status can generate (Collins, 1989). Yes, I could identify with hooks because I felt like an outsider in my own country. In describing her small-town Kentucky childhood, hooks notes, "living as we did – on the edge – we developed a particular way of seeing reality. We looked both from the outside and in from the inside out … we understood both" (hooks, 1984, p. 7). These words were written in America around the same time I felt like an outsider but, unlike hooks, I did not understand the proverbial standpoint – "look[ing] both from the outside and in from the inside out … [we] understood both" (1984, p. 7).

The reality I started developing was that my race meant that I was nothing, not even an afterthought. The feminist standpoint, according to Hartsock (1997, p. 368), "expresses female experience at a particular time and place, located within a particular set of social relations". Reading Hirschmarm's (1998) "Feminist standpoint as a postmodern strategy" several decades later, I came to realise that much like Erikson's theory of development, feminist standpoint theory does not account for the evolution of poststructuralist and postmodern thought. Yet, standpoint theory explained why my parents were so protective and did not want to talk about politics when I was eight years old. I simply would not understand, and, as a consequence, I felt no sense of psychological safety when I tried to make sense of our country's socio-political turmoil.

Psychological safety was crucial during the civil rights struggle because if any resistance strategy reached the armed forces, lives were at stake. Becoming a psychologist in post-apartheid South Africa, sitting in lecture halls listening to how the discipline of psychology contributed to my people feeling insecure, inferior and paranoid because of emotional insecurities harnessed during apartheid, defined my purpose.

Two of the greatest days of my life are the day I was born and the day I found out why I am here. I knew how I had to contribute to my country and beyond. The first step was to unravel what kind of person I was as a consequence of all the chronic trauma that we as black people experienced. Psychology started this civil war, designed and constructed by Verwoerd, an apartheid government prime minister and a psychologist who believed in setting limits on black education. So, as an ambitious undergraduate psychology major, I was bent on turning the discipline upside down to find answers.

Why didn't we feel secure? Psychologically safe? Why were we displaced, lost? But, most important, why didn't we feel like we belonged in the spaces that we occupied? What I did understand was that if Erikson's lifespan theory was to be the average identity developmental crisis, black people would mostly remain stuck in the inferior stage of development based on apartheid's aftermath. Yet, what my eight-year-old heart knew then was that I belonged in Rocklands, Mitchell's Plain, and that I identified with the people living in my community.

This was demonstrated by neighbours shamelessly borrowing a cup of sugar or coming over for tea unexpectedly. Most, if not all, the children on my block attended the same school. I fondly recall how we played "*kennetjie*". A street game that stands as a cultural symbol which cemented my sense of belonging to this community of people. The game represents some of the only entertainment we had. Since our parents could not afford to buy us toys, we made them ourselves.

A *kennetjie* is made from a small piece of wood and placed between two bricks. Whoever's turn it was, would take a longer piece of wood or a stick, and use it to hit the *kennetjie*, and the players would try to catch it. If you caught the *kennetjie* you won, and it was your turn to hit it with the stick. I can still hear the laughter, the air thick with excitement and overwhelming joy. Those were the good old days. It was fun, and no one was excluded. By the time the streetlights came on, we all said our goodbyes, ran home to wash up for dinner, and repeated the same routine the next day.

My mother's family also lived in Rocklands and I have very fond memories of my time with them, especially during the school holidays around Christmas-time. I grew up Anglican. That meant that it was a family tradition that on Christmas Eve, all the children would gather at my uncle's home while the parents went to Midnight Mass. When they returned, my cousin would have all the girls' hair in curlers, and we would unwrap presents together and eat donuts. My cousin, Anthea, made the best donuts in the world. We would go home in the early morning hours and return to my uncle's house for high tea which consisted of the best baked goods you could find. I really miss those days. I felt a strong sense of belonging and psychological security amongst my mother's family. During those occasions, politics were not discussed. I only recall laughter, smiles, closeness and people with whom I could identify.

After the holidays, everything would go back to normal: political meetings in our living-room, anti-apartheid strategies and political unrest. If there is one thing I know about myself, it is that I am good at blocking out painful memories. That is probably why the holidays with my mother's family in Rocklands meant so much to me. Their cheerful nature and warm-heartedness are what I will always hold near and dear because it blocked out the painful reality that our country was at war.

Boxing Day, the day after Christmas, is my parents' wedding anniversary and another family tradition was to go day camping somewhere remote. Since one of my uncles was in the navy, we always went to the most exclusive sites. Some of these camping sites had "whites-only" shops, and I remember my cousin being sent to the store because she is fair-skinned and has light – almost blonde – hair and could pass as white. I never understood what it meant (why I could not go into the shop with my cousin), but I never questioned it.

Becoming a psychologist in post-apartheid South Africa meant that I was able to make sense of why both boundaries and a sense of psychological safety ensured that members in my community felt a sense of belonging and shared a common identity. Picture this: neighbours standing in front of their gates shouting out stories across the way, having long conversations with each other about American soap operas; children playing *kennetjie*, jump rope and relentless laughter ringing in your ears. Having that feeling that you are accepted, consciously sensing that you are where you belong and feeling pride in your community, unsurprisingly identifying with being a member of Rocklands. Nonetheless, subconsciously knowing that this is the calm before the storm because of what was in the media – a cataclysmic country.

Cigarette smoke and Castle Lager beer fills my nostrils as I recall eavesdropping on the political meetings my father hosted in our living room. I was nine; old enough to be curious about the Casspirs roaming our streets, and the stench of tyres burning which left me wondering about what was happening in my community. I did not dare breathe or make a sound while I overhead my father talk about Mandela and Sisulu. About 15 years later, I worked with Sisulu's granddaughter at Howard University in Washington, DC, and she confirmed all my father's stories which made me smile out of sheer pride in my father's personal investment in the political struggle.

I remember telling my friend how I won an essay prize depicting my father's activist role. The topic was "What do you want to be when you grow up?" My essay was about the stories of political and economic struggle black people faced during apartheid and why I wanted to become a freedom activist. However, it dawned upon me while becoming a psychologist in post-apartheid South Africa that my childhood dreams would fade, and I would have to personally invest in a different type of struggle. Meanwhile my nine-year-old self was dealing with political unrest and blatant poverty, which still haunt me today.

Rewind to when I started school. Split-pea soup was a delicacy during breaktimes at Rocklands Primary School. My friends and I all went to the same preschool at Wembley, and we started Sub A (grade 1) in the same class. When the bell rang for first break, we ran to the soup line to buy a cup of split-pea soup for five cents. Most days I did not have five cents so my friends pooled money together, and I could join them in the soup line. When my father started to send money home from wherever he was, I did not need to run to the soup kitchen. I felt so ashamed eating the lunch my mother had prepared for me that I kept it a secret from my friends. To this day I love split-pea soup because the smell of the bone broth reminds me of the rocky times we endured and overcame in Rocklands.

I remember that politics was not the only struggle my family faced. One day my mother sent my younger sister and I to the local shop (we used to call it the "Bubby"). I was ten and my sister eight. The shop was two blocks away from our house. All the neighbours knew each other back then. As we were walking to the shop, people were screaming and we saw a mob of young men approaching us, fast. My heart was in my throat like a slippery sweet.

My sister grabbed my hand and squeezed it so tight that my fingers started to tingle. As the mob came closer, I heard gunshots. I did not know that they were gunshots then, but a neighbour saw how frozen and dazed we were, and she screamed, "Run home quickly!" It was too late. My sister and I were separated as the crowd ran through us. I screamed her name, but I could not see her, and I panicked.

I ran home hoping that she had done the same, but she had not. I was hysterical, sobbing uncontrollably. My mother was a wreck. She asked me where my sister was and I almost fainted because I was hoping that she was at home. My mother ran out to look for her. They returned a few moments later. My sister had been grabbed by a neighbour and kept safely in her home until the mob disappeared.

This was my first brush with gangsterism in Rocklands and my first experience of *ubuntu* (we are who we are because of others).

It was not long after the experience with those gangsters that my father returned home from Johannesburg. He told my mother that he was taking us away from the violence and the unrest. So, our plans to move to the rural Eastern Cape province (previously part of the Cape province and later regionally divided into the "independent" Transkei and Ciskei homelands) commenced. The next chapter will explore the interactive processes between the systemic levels of Bronfenbrenner's (2005) bioecology within the South African political front in the late 1980s. My father having to uproot his family to live in a different geographical location affected me deeply on the ecosystem dimension of the bioecological approach. In line with the microsystem sphere (person/individual system) I was not directly involved with my father's work environment at the time as his workplace was external to my experience; it nonetheless affected my development because of apartheid. We had to leave Cape Town because my father's work kept him away from us for much too long and he wanted to be with his family. According to Bronfenbrenner (1979), this explains the life-changing influence a parent's employment can have on a child's development.

3

Displacement and the worst day of my life

The look on her face when my father told my mother that we were leaving the Cape of Good Hope for the rural Ciskei is something I will never forget. Remember, my mom and her family were forcibly removed from District Six, then removed from Crawford and then displaced to Mitchell's Plain.

What my heart knows is that my mom, on that momentous day, was completely disheartened because her support system was in Rocklands. Mom had lost her parents before she turned eighteen. She was the youngest sibling and had taken their death the hardest.

On that day, I would have paid any price to take away my mother's fear, anxiety and deep sense of loss. What I remember about my mother most is that she was very close to her siblings and extended family. At nine years old I sensed that the unexpected plan my father presented to my mother made her feel lonely, unable to accept change and she experienced feelings of extreme loss. Then, it seemed to her as if her parents had died all over again because the familiar feeling of being forcibly removed had resurfaced, triggering feelings of unfairness and premature loss.

I never want to forget the time leading up to our inevitable move. In my heart of hearts, we were the perfect family, except that my parents were very secretive about the political unrest in our community and South Africa. Why did I believe them when they told me to put Vaseline on my face and to play under the bed when my eyes were burning because the neighbours were having a barbecue, setting off firecrackers and screaming because of birthday cheer? Today I know that the firecrackers were gunshots coming from army vehicles, the Vaseline was to protect me from the teargas and the screaming was not birthday cheer. It was my people screaming for their lives, being killed for hosting political meetings and protesting against the segregated policies which displaced us.

I'll never know why my father lied to me about what was happening in South Africa in the eighties. What I do know is that my father is a fearless protector of his family. I think he lied about what happened during apartheid because he wanted to preserve my childhood innocence for as long as possible. My dad is my hero. He is, but he could not protect me from everything. To this day my subconscious mind continues to shield me from the true horror of that fateful night.

The secret I'll take to my grave is who appeared in my bedroom one night in Rocklands.

I remember we were weeks away from moving to Ciskei. There were two family members who frequently visited on weekends because they were broke and my father provided food and shelter for them when they were in need.

That night, one of our visitors was under the influence of alcohol and my father was shouting at him because he was providing for them financially from the advance he had received from an American who had invested in him to start construction companies in the Ciskei. As I recall the most traumatic secret of my childhood, I feel a jolt that sends a shocking pain through my spine. This fearsome memory fills the air around me with the aroma of fried onion rings and calf's liver, a favourite delicacy of most people on a low budget around the Cape.

My sister and I shared a room in our two-bedroom rented house. Over the sound of the crackling onions and fried liver on the stove, my father instructed one of our visitors to go and sleep off his intoxication. He chose to get into my bed. Right now, I can still feel his strong arms wrapped tightly around me, feeling me up and down. His breath reeks of alcohol and smoke; I smell it even now. I can still feel his warm breath whisper in my ear: "Do you have a gown on?" Then my mind goes blank.

For the life of me, to this day, I do not know what happened next. I remember nothing. My subconscious clearly must have blocked it out because the episode was too traumatic. All I remember was that I wanted to scream but I could not breathe. In my mind I screamed "STOP!" but nothing was uttered, and I do not remember. I wish I could, but everything goes dark after my instant paralysis when he started touching me.

The childhood innocence my father so desperately tried to prolong was forcibly taken from me that catastrophic night. Childhood starts from birth to about 12 years according to developmental psychology, and I have taught this subject at various South African and American universities. However, in my experience, my childhood ended when I was physically and emotionally violated at 10 years old. Arguably, developmental psychology does not consider my experience and other girls like me who are violated and taken advantage of during the most vulnerable and voiceless periods of our growth and childhood innocence.

This poem comes closest to how I felt that frightful night:

I think back to when it happened,
think back to that awful night.
The night when it all happened,
the night he took "it" away.

Fighting. Yelling. Crying.
It didn't matter how loud I screamed.
Nobody came to help me.
Nobody came to set me free.

I still dream of running,
of trying to break away.
Of feeling him catch me,
every damn day.

I see him in the shadows,
even while I'm at home.
I close my eyes and pray he's gone,
only then I can't help but feel him.

To this day I feel him,
his tight grip on my wrists,
The pressure of his body
as I tried to resist.

He continued to thrust away,
as I fought and yelled and cried.
It didn't matter how loud I screamed,
Nobody came to help me.
Nobody came to set me free.
– Skinny Cow

You may still be thinking, "So, what's the secret?" The secret that I will take to my grave is the identity of the perpetrator. He is too powerful, highly respected, and very well connected for my voice to ever count against his. He is "family". It is this reality that drew me to psychology. This childhood secret was hidden away in the cobwebs of my mind until one day in an abnormal psychology class, my lecturer activated my brain cells that triggered this memory when describing a case study which resembled my experience. Now this case study was my life, and it drew me closer to the need to become a psychologist. I wanted to become a psychologist while sitting in that class so badly because I wanted to know more about myself and I wanted to heal, mend the broken pieces of the puzzle of what happened to me in that bed when I was ten years old. I wanted to help girls like me. I wanted to understand what happened during apartheid and why? I wanted to clean out the cobwebs in my muddled mind.

This red-flag moment in abnormal psychology was a flashback, post-traumatic moment that took my breath away. Those were the moments that counted. Since then I've known that the only way to catch my breath and make my voice count was to become a critical (applied) health psychologist.

4

Bad times in Breidbach

Enter the horrific season of an unfathomable experience that changed everything. My father went ahead of us to Breidbach, King William's Town, to set up house and shop. My mother, sisters and I took an 11-hour bus trip to Breidbach. The bus dropped us off at the entrance of Breidbach in the middle of the night. We had to cross a dark, short bridge to get into the neighbourhood. This small suburb of King William's Town is in the Eastern Cape province and occupied predominantly by isiXhosa- and Afrikaans-speaking black people (the latter also known as "coloureds").

We slept at my great aunt's house because she lived near the entrance to Breidbach. When we got to the house, we took a bath and went straight to bed.

The next morning, my father and his family came to welcome us. Since it was the end of the academic year, everyone was excited to know how we did in our final exams. One of my father's younger brothers called my cousin and I, who were the same age, and asked to see our report cards. What I cannot write about is who this uncle is because his behaviour began a downward spiral that would shatter my self-esteem.

I had always got straight As and my parents were so proud of me. However, coming from Cape Town, the grand total of my marks was 327 out of 330, whereas my cousin, who went to Breidbach Primary School, had a total 328 out of 330. I will never forget the disgust on my uncle's face because I got one mark lower than my cousin.

My first bad memory of my uncle was him shouting at me for being stupid enough not to get full marks in all my subjects. These were some of the hateful remarks that are now be branded into my soul.

As the years went by living in Breidbach I was constantly told that I was just not good enough. I tried to be perfect because I would never erase the contempt in my uncle's eyes and the glee on my cousin's face. I recall this experience as the beginning of the worst five years of my young life.

When we lived in Breidbach I was plagued by thoughts of whether it would even be possible to move on from the bad times. Whether I'd be able to find true joy and contentment in my life again.

I remember feeling scared, shy and anxious on my first day of school. My teachers were amazing, but the children were horrible. The boys would hit me on my head and say things like "Your hair is so thick; it feels like a pillow."

This is how deep-rooted racist undercurrents infiltrated the psyches of young black boys. In terms of beauty standards, straight hair and fair skin are what black people have been measured against. Who would have known that later in my life I would be so affected by this that I would publish research in peer-reviewed scientific journals on how magazines depict ethnically sanitised versions of black women. In other words, black models with chemically straightened hair and bleached skin would be used in magazine advertisements to appeal to the male gaze in order to standardise perceptions of beauty at a subliminal level.

But the girls were the worst! There was a clique that wanted me to join them. Think of the 2004 movie *Mean Girls* – but on steroids. I was not interested in playing with them, so they beat me up every day, as well as anyone who came close to being kind to me. Picture this: on any given day, four to six of the most popular girls at school standing in a line during recess scrutinising me from about a metre away. Staring me down, laughing, taunting, waiting and watching to see if anyone would approach me. There was one relentless girl who kept checking on me and, as soon as they spotted her talking to me, she had to run, and I got a smack.

No one was supposed to get near me. If I did not want to hang out with them, I did not have their permission to talk to anyone else. So, each day during recess I would take out my library book and read. I held my book up so that they could not see my face. Sometimes I would peer over my Nancy Drew book to check if they were still watching me and if they spotted me doing that, they would start calling me names and taunting me. Books were my safe space, so I just hid behind them.

One day after months of torture, I just started to cry when I woke up. I begged my mother to not send me to school. I begged to go back to Cape Town. I told her what was going on at school, so she and my father went to see the principal. I remember that at first, he did not want to believe me. These girls were so popular that they had the teachers wrapped around their pinkies. One was the daughter of a wealthy businessman, another was the daughter of one of the teachers at the school, yet another was a star athlete and one of them was a fearless fighter on the playground. They used the fearless fighter to do all the physical abuse of course. So, each one had a purpose.

After several days of my parents having lengthy meetings with each of my teachers, I returned to class. That is when the bullying got worse. I got beaten up for telling on them. Worst part: the teacher who was the father of one of the girls sat her next to me in class – likely in an ironic bid to forge a friendship between us by force of and proximity. She would pinch me so hard underneath the desk and dare me to cry. I fought back tears and tried to hide the blue and red marks on my body.

Why did I not fight back? If I did, they would threaten to gang up on me after school or during break. So, all I could do was bow my head in painful silence and allow my books to transport me to anywhere but there. (Ironically, some of them would later send me a friend request on Facebook – the horror of cyberbullying.) But books saved me from the bad experiences in Breidbach.

I hugged my Nancy Drew books as I made my way through the library exit, with happy thoughts of how I would not sleep until I had read at least three chapters. I smiled. Could I have known then that my favourite place in the entire Eastern Cape (besides the beach), would also become the place I most dreaded to visit after a very traumatic experience?

Let's pause here for a moment and shift the focus to a biopsychosocial model of health and well-being initially proposed by George Engel (1981) and developed by Bronfenbrenner (1979). It provides a basis for exploring the interconnections between a child's physical and mental health, their access to resources and the social setting in which they live and grow, and their behaviour to suggest how risks to these indicators of wellbeing may positively or negatively affect their development. It also highlights the embeddedness of the individual, social institutions and societal ideologies in influencing the development of children, and adults. To support the investigation into my family's move from the big city of Cape Town, to the rural confines of Breidbach, it leans on the Bronfenbrenner model to support the understanding of my well-being and development as a child. Within the borders of the Eastern Cape's rural encapsulated boundaries, movement was dictated by apartheid laws. Everything about my identity leading up to the move was a drastic change and a shift happened. My first language is English but the rural area we moved to was purely Afrikaans which limited my interaction with everyone in this new geographical area because they all spoke Afrikaans. The amount of times I was ostracised because I responded to an Afrikaans question in English was brutal. Constant trauma for being-in-this-world as a black, English-speaking city girl definitely influenced my emotional, social and intellectual development. When a child is trying to navigate through constant turmoil they either develop a sense of resilience, that is, the capacity of a system to adapt successfully to challenges that threaten the function, survival or future development of the system. Unless development is dysfunctional, resilience across system levels and its applicability to resilience in a person, a family, a healthcare system, a community, an economy, or other systems, is required. According to Bronfenbrenner (2005), to explore the interactive processes within the systemic levels lends an explanation of what affects child development on the person dimension of the bioecological approach. The mesosystem (e.g. my religion) affected my ability to build resilience when I was hopeless. For example, throughout his trials in the Old Testament (Job 19: 25–27, New International Version), Job found hope in and rooted himself in God's character and promises. Job constantly reminds us of God's love. I developed resilience because I believe that God is my ultimate redeemer. Regardless of how circumstances changed in my life, God is the one who ultimately rescued me in the end. After suffering passes, God will still remain. This is the hope that I hold onto, always.

I was 14 or 15 years old at the time. According to Erikson (1956) and most developmental theorists (Schultz & Lawrence, 2017), during this stage of my life, that is, adolescence, my peers would have the most significant influence on my life. The psychosocial modality of being oneself and sharing oneself is prominent in this stage of development. If one is to consider peer pressure and bullying, I would renounce Erikson's (1956) notion that maladaptation at this stage is repudiation. The area in which a psychobiography mostly engages the psyche of an individual is through personality development. Between the ages of 12 to 18 years, my peers bullied me.

Here is a case in point. Walking out of the library minutes before it closed, out of the blue, someone from school put her arm around my shoulder and asked me to come with her to the bathroom before I went home. There were the twins: Samuel and Samson! They had a major crush on me. She had tricked me. Samuel shoved me into one of the bathroom cubicles and forced me to kiss him. How disgusting! My stomach churned. I would have thrown up in his mouth had he came any closer. Sam screamed for help because I was putting up a fight. Samson barged into the cubicle and held both my hands apart to make space for both to kiss me. I felt powerless, violated and I was screaming for help. The librarian heard me and, had it not been for her, who knows what they would have done to me.

This started a painful pattern of pubescent boys trying to violate me physically. I did not feel safe. Girls thought I was seducing their boyfriends. Meanwhile, their boyfriends were forcing themselves on me and, dare I say, nearly assaulting me sexually. I got beaten up by so many girls in Breidbach I lost count. Little did the jealous girlfriends know that to their boyfriends I was this new plaything from the city, and the boys just wanted to have fun. Consequently, I was synonymous with a harlot, spat on and bullied, isolated, and called horrific names I just want to forget.

Psychobiography goes beyond the facts of my life. It seeks to interpret the psychological meaning of those facts. I describe the psychobiography method in the final section of this book. For now, I'm using snippets of the methodological framework to give examples of how this autopsychobiography helps me make meaning of my lived experience as a child.

Autosychobiography calls for perspicacity, the ability to make psychological connections, basically, interpreting my lived experience through a psychological lens.

Here is another example of how I interpret my truth. One day I was sitting in class doing my work. One of the fearsome foursome walked over to me and put a note in my pocket. I was so afraid to move that I was sweating profusely. When the teacher left the room, a boy walked up to me and took the note out of my pocket. I felt so helpless and violated. I was completely unprepared for what followed.

He called the class's attention to me and said: "Look what I found in her pocket". Then he started reading out loud: "Dear Liezille, thank you for having sex with me in the bathroom while you were waiting for your ride home. It was awesome. You were amazing."

I was 12. I had not even menstruated yet. I had not yet had the birds and the bees talk from my mother. So, naturally, I was shocked. I almost cried but I did not dare move. The entire class was laughing and everyone started calling me names. This is how vicious rumours about me started to spread. When we would change classes, I would see my name written on school benches alongside hideous sexist graffiti.

That letter burnt a hole in my soul because I could not imagine having sex at 12. I did not even know what sex was. I just knew it was something forbidden at my age. How could they even put that to paper and frame me in that way? Those girls were the meanest, but they sure did prepare me for what I was faced with later in my life. Mean girls grow up and become mean adults. Becoming a psychologist, I was trained by and brushed shoulders with similar mean girls in the discipline but more about that later. Framing this experience and how it influenced my personality development, it is important to note where I positioned myself in terms of Erikson's psychosocial development theory. Erikson developed this lifespan theory from a man's viewpoint. Meaning that his theory tends to describe how adolescent boys develop identity which in my opinion is very different to how adolescent girls develop. Critics (Curry, 1998) of Erikson's (1968) theory indicate that female identity development is typically focused more on relationships and relating to others (like forming cliques). So, when young adolescent girls establish their identities, they depend heavily on social relationships (Curry, 1998).

The biopsychosocial model systematically considers biological, psychological and social factors, and their complex interactions in understanding mental health (Engel, 1977). At this age my body was undergoing puberty; psychologically I was being violated through social factions at school and after school by cousins who only spoke Afrikaans. There's a case to make here that I was at a developmental crossroad and needed to build resilience to survive. According to Bronfenbrenner's systems theory of bioecology, my developmental trajectory was pushing me to develop self-awareness, mindfulness, self-care and positive relationships in order to build my character. I needed to learn to speak Afrikaans and make friends. I enjoyed spending time with myself. Reading and writing letters to my friends in Cape Town was my favourite pastime. Needless to say, it took a lot of alone time to assimilate into my new environment.

Given that, ethnically, black people develop a sense of identity differently to white people, I recall that in the early years of my own development I overheard the first lady of our country label me as "*a non-person*" (Maja-Pearce, 1994, p. 135). This affected me so much because I could not see the person as I was listening to her voice over the radio. I also never really saw white people when I was growing up because of apartheid's segregation laws. All I knew were black people. So, in my teenage mind, I thought, a non-person meant that I did not exist. That I should be invisible. This is how my identity started to take shape. I tried to make myself invisible because someone important on the radio had said that my kind were non-persons.

In high school I rebelled. I used to run away from school so often that my father's cousin, who still works at the high school today, called him to tell on me. He meant well but I just wanted to escape. Ironically, that little bridge at the entrance to Breidbach is where I spent most of my days. Hiding from the horny boys and bullies.

I remember that my parents were so upset with my rebellion they called in my father's two educated brothers for back-up. They wanted to send me to stay with the one in Cape Town, but he refused. The one in Breidbach was funny. He came into my room with a hilarious look on his face. He said: "Liezille your parents are concerned about this naughtiness of yours. If you stop running away from school, I promise to send you to one of the progressive English schools in town."

Obviously, he was lying because it was during apartheid and we were not allowed to mix with white children in "progressive schools", whatever that meant. I nonetheless started going back to school because my father threatened to send me to work in a factory shop in Cape Town. School was a chaotic mess anyway – boycotts, sit-ins, chalk-downs. We were not even getting regular classes at one point. Also, our time in Breidbach was running out because my father was betrayed by the people closest to him.

I do a good job of blocking out painful memories but what I can write about is a few things that I learned from living in Breidbach.

My sister and I had to go to an Afrikaans school because back then those were the only schools for black people in Breidbach. We had been taught only in English in Cape Town, so we had to do our homework and study using dictionaries in Breidbach. I did not even know my subject names in Afrikaans. My paternal cousins told us that their parents were hoping we would fail and keep repeating grades. To their chagrin, we had built up resilience in Rocklands and so were determined to succeed – we passed every grade right through to high school in an Afrikaans-medium institution.

I learned to appreciate reading and started writing letters to pen pals all over the country. I spent most of my free time at the library because I had almost no friends. Books became my friends because the stories transported me to a place and time far away from the hell I was living through.

I was bullied a lot in Breidbach. I just did not fit in and felt like I was misplaced, as if I did not belong there. Every night I would pray to the Heavenly Father to forgive the bullies and begged God to make them stop. It was only later in my career that I realised how being bullied had built up a kind of fortitude in me. I can spot a bully a mile away and quickly adjust my disposition into flight or fight mode. Being bullied isolated me. I think this is partly why I am a loner. I enjoy being by myself, reading and writing. I remember reading the Bible a lot as a child and I still do.

My father is a hero. Every Saturday morning he would round us up in his 16-seater van and take us to a wholesaler where he would buy in bulk, ask us to help him make food parcels and then go to the areas where unemployment was rife. My father would knock on doors, and hand over huge food parcels which could possibly last an entire family for the week. He did this every week and I witnessed this with great admiration.

My father taught me that even though I was miserable in Breidbach we were there to do good. My father lived his purpose. He taught me how to be benevolent. There were little to no recreational activities in Breidbach. So, my father started a soccer club enrolling all the young men he employed in his various construction companies. He even started a girl's football club of which I was the goalkeeper.

I remember that just before we left King William's Town my father participated in the protest march that would come to be known as the Bisho Massacre of 1992. The protest was about demands to end the military rule in the then Ciskei Bantustan. Daddy was one of 8 000 led by Cyril Rhamaposa, amongst other ANC leaders. Rifles, hand grenades and machine guns opened fire for five minutes non-stop. Dad said it felt like five hours. My dad was not injured but he used his 16-seater to transport injured women and children to Frere Hospital. He took it upon himself to transport casualties of this massacre to the hospital which he described as being a blood bath. The terrifying image of my father drenched in the blood of women and children, and the smell of their blood, still lingers as I evoke the memory of this cataclysmic event.

The Bisho Massacre was the beginning of my family's distress. People in his companies, people he considered to be close to him, people he trusted, stole from him. They stole his clients; stole the company's money and he was declared bankrupt. This resulted in my father having three consecutive heart attacks. When he healed, we moved back to Cape Town and he was appointed as a residence manager at the University of the Western Cape (UWC). I was sixteen.

5

Living in two dimensions

No higher education institution reflects the complex and diverse history of higher education in South Africa quite like the three flagship universities of the current Western Cape. The University of the Western Cape, established during the apartheid era, has a history of opposition to that oppressive regime and, since the country's transition to democracy, has been focused on transforming its role in the South Africa of today (Wolpe, 1995). Stellenbosch University, historically an Afrikaans institution, has been associated with the promotion of Afrikaner culture and language (Bickford-Smith, 1995). The oldest of the three, the University of Cape Town has, like Stellenbosch University, been known for excluding black students under apartheid and operating as an exclusive, eltist English, Anglo-Saxon and colonial space.

In 1993, my father started working at the University of the Western Cape or UWC, also known as the "University of Left", also known as the "Bush". We lived on campus. It was a huge adjustment, yet for the first time in my teenage life I did not feel displaced. I felt a strong sense of belonging.

Although a student residence is not an ideal home in which to raise four children, I absolutely loved it. It felt like my home was a huge mansion with an Olympic-size swimming pool, tennis and squash courts, track and field, the list goes on.

The highlight of living at UWC was access to the library at the age of 16. I was in book heaven. My favourite authors were and still are Socrates, Descartes and other philosophical pioneers like Nietzsche. Among radical leftists, I could hold my own in discussions on politics and sociological constructs that affect our being-in-the-world. On the one hand, I was an awkward teenager navigating through high school and, on the other hand, I was an eager teenager ready to start student life.

According to Erikson (1968a), I was having an identity crisis which contributed to my awkward phase. The influence my new university-aged friends had on my social and personality development contributed to the complexities I experienced as a teenager. My father was very strict and did not want us fraternising with the students. However, he had a few students he favoured and whom we were permitted to befriend, mostly young men. They were what my siblings and I called our "father's watch dogs".

Living at UWC before April 1994 was a reprieve from what was happening around us and in the rest of the country. But the students were quick to remind us that even though the doors of learning were open, we were not free. Tyres burning at the main entrance to the university, sit-ins, protests about finance, and the protests at the main administration buildings brought back memories of the hair-raising times in Rocklands. At one point, my father and his colleagues were held hostage by the student protesters until their demands were met. Like the #FeesMustFall movement of 2015–2016, UWC students were relentless. Before I even enrolled as a student at the university, I was made aware that UWC produces critical thinkers, freedom fighters and the type of cadre you will never find on any other campus in South Africa or perhaps the world. Resilience, endurance, no one left behind, commitment to the political struggle and the academic project. I learned all of this as a high school student.

According to Shultz (2005), during the first five stages of our psychosocial development we are exposed by our parents, teachers, peer groups and various opportunities which are entirely out of our control. For example, moving from Cape Town to Breidbach was my father's decision. Moving to UWC while I was a teenager was also my father's decision. Growing up in Mitchell's Plain, Breidbach and on a university campus affected my attitude towards life and built strengths formed during the early stages of my life.

When campus was quiet at the end of the year and students had gone home for recess, our high school friends would visit and we would take them on tours of the university, imagining what it would be like to study there. Sadly, I was one of two or three of my entire matric class who made it to university. I attended a school people in the area called "Gangster High", again a recommendation from a family member who was a teacher. She told my mother that this was the best school close to UWC, yet she sent her own children to a middle-class school.

I will never forget the first day of school. When my dad dropped off my younger sister and I, we stood back-to-back like we were in a shoot-out, surrounded by murderers, and it was about to go down. The profanity learners were shouting at each other, the gold teeth and the tattoos were out of a movie. Again, we were petrified.

As time went by, we got used to the vileness of the children and our friends pointed out what they called "*die moordenaars*" (the murderers), who were obviously gangsters. Our only way to survive in Gangster High was to not make eye contact with them. Luckily, we survived – barely.

Walking home from school alone one day I was crossing the bridge on my way to campus when a guy pulled over and casually told me that my father sent him to pick me up. I had never met him, so I politely declined. This man pulled me into his car and started talking to me like we had known each other for years. He asked me if I was thirsty, and I nodded; meanwhile I could not breathe. When he stopped at the shop, there were a lot of pupils from my school in and outside the shop. He gave me R10 and said I should go and get the drink; he would wait outside for me. The entire time I could not breathe. One of the girls saw the terror in my eyes and asked me if I was okay. I asked if I could walk with her and her friends to escape this man who had just abducted me. She was horrified and hid me so that he could not see me. I took a different route home and luckily never ran into this man again.

As I write this, I'm filled with a deep sadness and transported to a time of confusion and shock. I take an intensely deep breath, shaking my head and wondering what I would have told my 17-year-old self then. I want to travel back in time and tell her to hang in there. Once you become a psychologist, all the pieces of the muddled puzzle will fit into place – well, eventually. I would tell my teenage self that it would not get better but that I would build mental and emotional fortitude. This highlights an important critique of Erikson's theory because he does not adequately explain how emotional development takes place in life (Louw, 1998). The emotional grit I developed from early childhood to this point has created a determined and tenacious perseverance within me.

When I started my last year of high school, my parents were concerned about what I would study at UWC. Note: not *if* I would study but *what*. I was predestined to become a leftist and UWC was the obvious choice. My father and mother were mortified when I told them that I wanted to study journalism. They sent me to the student counselling centre at UWC. It turned out that I was to become a psychologist after all. I knew nothing about the discipline other than that, apparently, you sit in a room with someone telling you their problems and you offer advice. That seemed boring because I wanted to have a greater sense of purpose than psychology's seemingly individualistic approach. However, I decided to give it a shot.

Meanwhile, I was observing what it would be like to be a student. I categorised students into two groups: the change makers and the party animals. I failed to understand why the party animals would waste their parents' money and their own time when we were at the dawn of our liberation. Becoming a psychologist gave me insight into the reasons why most students partied so hard. People have different coping strategies. There was and still is a huge amount of pressure on black students to succeed and improve their lives.

I will never forget all the suicides my father had to report to parents every year during June and November exams. He walked to Unibell, a train station behind the university, to identify his students' bodies. My dad believed that suicide was contagious because one year there were more than 30 suicides in his residence. That was the straw that broke the camel's back. He had to begin long-term therapy because he was very fond of all his students and knew them all personally.

My father hated feminists. One day during the December holidays a female student came to our home attached to the residence. I was watching TV, so I was within earshot of the conversation. I do not recall the story vividly but what I do remember is that she demanded to stay in her old room with her baby because she had no place to go. I remember my father telling her that her room was occupied by vacation visitors and that she was not allowed on campus until she could register for the new academic year. She was disrespectful, hysterical and the baby started crying so my father called security to escort her off campus. When campus reopened, she made a harassment case against my father and our family was left without income for three months. She was represented by a feminist group on campus, and this accounts for my father's disdain for feminists.

I felt that my father was treated unfairly. Yet, I also knew that what these women expressed was misandry, not feminism.

All these experiences on campus before I was even a registered student shaped the reasons why becoming a feminist and a critical psychologist were so important to me. As I reflect on my greatest struggles during my early years, I realise that they gave birth to my greatest triumphs. I remember with a twinkle in my eye and a smile how my father cried when I read this paragraph to him.

6

A university orientation

My palms were sweaty. My heart was racing. There were just too many people, and it was too noisy. It was first-year orientation day. I was sandwiched between my parents on the bleachers at UWC's stadium. The rector was about to welcome the first years and our parents to the university. I was anxious because I was about to embark on a journey with thousands of what was dubbed South Africa's first "free" black professionals.

This is the story I want to write about in this chapter because it is worth telling. I want to pull back the curtain a bit to remind people of what was riding on the first years sitting in that stadium at UWC on that day in 1995, the first full academic year of our country's new democracy. I want to pull back the curtain and expose the innovative pedagogy demonstrated by our lecturers to make sure that we would not let them down.

One could taste the anticipation and suspense as it was projected by the high-spirited and colourful vibrations of the UWC choir. I remember one thing about the speech the rector made that day. It was very encouraging yet drenched in melancholy. He emphasised that we were standing on the shoulders of cadres who fought fervently for our freedom, who made it possible for us to live out our dreams like no other black person could before us. We were commanded to prove the struggle was not in vain. Becoming a professional, a critical psychologist in the new South Africa was *expected*; this differs from Manganyi's (2013) experience described in *On Becoming a Psychologist in Apartheid South Africa*.

Allow me to give you a front row seat to what becoming a critical psychologist in post-apartheid South Africa was like, for me at least. What I cannot write about is what the atmosphere was like at the beginning of the academic year at UWC; it is indefinable. As a teenager, I had lived on campus, so I already had a sneak peek into orientation week. However, as an 18-year-old first-year student living in university residence with my parents and siblings, it was uncanny. If you were me, you would want to write a letter to your teenage self about what was unfolding. Even though I thought I had the upper hand because campus had been my playground for at least three years before I became a student at UWC, I was in for a rude awakening.

After all the formalities and see-you-laters to our parents, the Student Counselling's Peer Facilitator Programme took over. The first years were grouped into their different faculties and then divided into smaller groups of less than 20, each with a peer facilitator (PF). I can still remember that I wore a peach-coloured skirt, and the grass was making my legs itch because I was sweating like a sinner in church on Sunday. Not only was it hot but I think I had a case of moderate social anxiety. There were so many of us. I saw a sea of starry eyes and hopeful, "We made it" smirks, still coming off the high of the "sky's the limit for your generation" speeches and proud looks on our parents' faces.

The subjects I enrolled in were majors in Psychology and Philosophy with Anthropology and Sociology, Linguistics and English as arbitraries.

I will never forget Sam. She sat behind me in the scorching sun waiting on our peer facilitator to make sure she got all our contact details and that we all had the necessary documents with us. Sam did not look cheerful at all. She told me that she was a "legacy". Both her parents went to UWC. Her father was still working there as a professor. She looked very sad, but I did not want to probe. I was dealing with my own social anxieties.

I did not mind crowds but there was a limit to how long I could tolerate being in such a noisy environment. The peer facilitators were oozing with energy as if they had been waiting all their lives for this very moment. When I looked around me, I saw a rainbow of bright brown faces and that I was not the only one sweating from the heat and anxiety. I think to a great extent, many of us had mixed emotions.

Once everybody was signed up for orientation by our peer facilitator, we left the stadium to find a tree to sit under and get to know each other through various icebreakers and games. These exercises calmed my nerves a bit and I felt a bit more relaxed by the end of the day.

I am an introvert. I need solitude to regain my energy and recharge. However, walking home after a long day filled with anxiety and uneasiness was unsettling. Students had thrown a huge party in front of the parking area adjacent to our campus-residence home. Inside the residence were welcome-back parties. I was even invited to a few.

All I remember was that I wanted to read my favourite Deepak Chopra book and call it a night.

When I walked through the front door my family was excited to hear how my first day had been and how many new friends I had made. I immediately thought about Sam. During the icebreakers and games, she and I were partners. She was technically my first friend at UWC. She told me that her mother had died a year ago and that her grandmother had just passed away. She also had a twin brother who had committed suicide. She was from Fairways, a high- to middle-class community in Cape Town. She even had her own car. I was shocked because I could not even drive then. Yet she was so troubled. "You remind me of ..." I started saying but stopped mid-sentence because I did not want her to know how troubled I was too. Although we were about to start a new and exciting chapter both our past experiences still haunted us.

The 1995 orientation at UWC was a moment that will forever be marked in time. In my mind was a time capsule of the period before I existed: colonialism and the beginning of apartheid. A time I am tethered to because of my parents' lived experience. Given the backdrop of our nation's new democracy and the uncertainty of what university life would be like for the first "free" psychologists – life before, life now – is it even possible to conceive of a more momentous occasion? I did not comprehend the magnitude of how politically charged UWC was until I became a student. There were so many political parties, rivals even, and they were all black people fighting with each other. I was so confused. My naivety about the politics and ethnocentrism in South Africa was overwhelming. Constant rallies and protests on campus were the norm. When you heard the infamous chants, *"Hek toe!"* (March to the main gate), you knew tyres were about to burn and forceful demands were about to be made by students. Even though there were opposition parties, they all agreed on one fundamental truth and that was *"A luta continua"* (The struggle continues).

As a student body we were made aware via the *Student Voice* news-paper, campus radio and politically charged posters that there was a list of demands that needed to be addressed in higher education. If I could write a letter to my 18-year-old self I would say freedom came at a price and 20 years down the line you will still be grappling with transformation in higher education.

All universities were not equal in 1995. Down the road from UWC, Stellenbosch University was still teaching in Afrikaans, which meant that you were excluded from the university if you did not have an aptitude for the language. UWC probably had one per cent or fewer white students. More importantly, we did not have equal access to educational resources compared with universities like Stellenbosch and the University of Cape Town had, for example. So, our lecturers overcompensated. They used Euro-American texts to teach us by contextualising the work in a South African setting in attempts to redress the transformative shortcomings in the curriculum. Even though we were taught from Euro-American texts, the history of the discipline was magnified in a sense that we were not technically "free" until we had equal access to educational resources.

Some scholars believe that personal growth and development is an outcome of freedom, yet education enables this development. However, this begs the question: How do we re-historicise the university curriculum in South Africa to reconstruct a coherent and concrete radical curriculum rendering all universities equal?

"Who smokes marijuana? Raise your hand. Who smokes cigarettes? Who drinks alcohol? Who drinks coffee and has never quit?" Everyone's hand is raised. "You you are all illustrating symptoms of addictive behaviour," said Rafiq Lockhart, laughing out loud. He was the first psychology lecturer who addressed our first-year class. I will never forget the roaring laughter and gasps coming from the classroom packed with first-year psychology students. My hair stood on end and a lump formed in my throat because surely drinking coffee did not mean that I was an addict. What would my parents say if they found out? At that moment I got hooked on psychology.

The next psychology class he walked through the door and asked: "What's your favourite sitcom?" Someone shouted: "Friends!" He shouted back: "Why, does it remind you of your friends or would you like to have friends like Rachel, Monica or Chandler?" Everyone laughed. Psychology challenged us to think about everyday life through a critical lens. "Am I in heaven?" That is what I kept asking myself. Every lecture brought me closer to understanding a little bit more about why I and those around me behave the way we do. Personality, Abnormal, Developmental, and Research were my favourite psychology modules.

7

Flashbacks and a "new" father

One day in class the air turned black all around me. A shrill cry echoed in my mind. Blurry-eyed, I finally regained control of my senses. My Abnormal Psychology lecturer transported me to a place and time in my life that made my hair stand on end again. Once more I heard footsteps staggering towards the bedroom I shared with my younger sister. The door handle turned slowly. I felt uneasy, almost as if death lurked at the door. At age 19 I could still feel his icy fingers gripping my arm in the darkness.

I felt like I had killed my ten-year-old self that fateful night. After class I went to my favourite secluded spot in the library and cried my heart out. I just sat there sobbing quietly for hours.

The lecturer was telling us about a case he was working on. A young girl around nine or ten was molested by her father's brother. He, the uncle, was under the influence of alcohol. The difference between me and his client was that she had screamed, and her parents rushed to the room. She went for therapy. This little girl had been way more courageous than I was at her age. Yet, almost 30 years later, I've built enough endurance, fortitude and courage to tell my story to the world without a shred of fear in my heart.

Little did the lecturer know that while he was standing behind the podium reading through his case notes from an overhead transparency that he was triggering feelings of trauma that were hidden deep in my subconscious.

Often at the beginning of my lectures, I warn students that what I say or may ask them has the potential to trigger feelings of past trauma. I advise them to read the course outline which provides them with prescribed texts well in advance for them to be prepared in the event that the material might trigger a reaction. I advise them to leave the classroom, go to student counselling or just go somewhere quiet where they can collect their thoughts and decide on the way forward. I want to emphasise that there were no trigger warnings when I was trained in psychology. Upon reflection, I believe that psychology is meant as a trigger for us to heal – ready or not – which should probably be a disclaimer in our undergraduate course handbooks.

There was more to becoming a psychologist than sitting in lecture halls and completing assessments. In my second year I signed up to be a peer facilitator during orientation and then a mentor later that same year. For this I received leadership training from therapists at student counselling. This was the beginning of personal growth, of building self-esteem and learning how to go beyond my comfort zone. People always say that university is the prime of one's life. I do not think that it is the only such peak, but I will say that I did more community engagement work in the first four years of university than I had done in my life up until then. I loved every moment because each project enriched the lives of others and gave me a deeper sense of who I was and what my purpose was and could be as a critical psychologist.

My father as residence manager at UWC had me involved in all his community service work. Every Wednesday night we would go to a boys' home and do life-skills building and give life-orientation workshops. At weekends we would help by taking kids from the surrounding areas in Belhar and Bellville South to the beach, or do indoor activities with them that encouraged personal development and growth. What I gained from these encounters no Euro-American psychology textbook could teach me. *Ubuntu* might be a broad reach to what Vygotsky (2012), a Russian psychologist, coined sociocultural learning theory. Nonetheless, community engagement was a real boost to my personal growth. I will always be grateful for the exposure to community service led by my father and his house committee members.

When I referred to my relationship to my father in previous chapters it was from the viewpoint of my early childhood. Upon reflection, he appeared as a man who had been an absent father for most of my younger years. But I understood his absence as the result of working to provide for his family. My earliest memories of my father were of when we lived in Rocklands and the role he played in the country's struggle against apartheid (Chapter 2). Vivid memories of a more unstable relationship with my father from the time we lived in Breidbach (Chapter 4) would gradually emerge with time. It was then that my relationship with my father began to weaken. I'd begun to notice his drinking problem.

My father was not always a saint. He had alcohol use disorder. On many nights students would bring him home staggering from the Barn, the campus watering hole. This started huge arguments between my parents and as children we knew that we needed to get out of the way and be quiet. When he was under the influence of alcohol, all the things he noticed that irritated him when he was sober were rehashed and amplified. My father never beat my mother. He had us for that. He had an extremely stressful job, and it was difficult for him to take orders since he had overseen his own businesses for so long.

I hated what alcohol did to my father. I feared for my life. That is how blind his rage could be when he was under the influence of alcohol. Every night before going to bed, I would pray that he would not kill me in my sleep.

This experience and other addictive behaviours encountered through my extended family led me to a career in substance use disorder research. My doctoral thesis (Pretorius, 2010) was titled "Women's discourses about secretive alcohol dependence and experiences of accessing treatment", and it jump-started my research career as a critical health psychology and gender studies scholar.

I belonged to the Anglican Students Society (ANSOC) at UWC and served for two terms as the Gender Equality Officer. ANSOC also engaged in various community service projects such as creating awareness campaigns on HIV/Aids.

Our main annual event was my favourite. On one occasion, we visited a creepy convent near the Lesotho border. It was in the heart of winter. The ANSOC steering committee and a few members, led by our chaplain, Father Courtney Sampson, my favourite Anglican priest, huddled up into a 16-seater and drove all the way from Cape Town to a national university retreat. The convent had no electricity or warm water. So, for a city slicker like me, it was eerie, at the risk of sounding sacrilegious. Yet it was exciting to meet so many different people who came from all over the country representing their universities. There was a huge, beautifully designed church building, and a massive great hall where meals and workshops took place.

During one of our workshops, a nun was teaching us the significance of prayer. We discussed and unpacked why we should address God as a man, that is, "Our Heavenly Father". During this period my father was a binge drinker and very violent. "So how could God possibly be a man?" I boldly asked the nun. What proof was there in the scripture that God was male? She told me to see her after the workshop because she had a lot to cover in a short space of time with our group.

After the workshop I went to her and the first thing she asked me was: "What is your relationship with your father like?" I was taken aback. I did not expect her to go straight for the jugular. I was at a loss for words, and she could tell. She told me to go find a quiet place and think about it. She told me that she would be available to answer any questions I had following my reflection, or even if I just wanted her to listen.

I did go to her eventually and during that conversation I discovered that my relationship with my earthly father hindered a deeper connection with my Creator. I had a lot of soul searching to do and the retreat was the best place to start. My reflections on my father and his struggle with alcohol dependency were painful but necessary for my development. Still, it was a long and painful journey to understand addiction and make peace with my father.

I finally had a breakthrough when my father volunteered to book himself into a treatment facility. This coincided with my doctoral studies – listening to women's accounts of their secretive alcohol addictions. When the women in my study told their life stories about the first time they picked up a drink until they reached recovery within the Alcoholics Anonymous fraternity, only then did I finally make peace with my father and start mending our relationship.

I understood my father on a deeper level than merely at that of our father–daughter relationship. I gained insight into his condition and that deepened our connection.

Before I became a critical health psychologist, I did not have a good relationship with my father, and I often yearned for father figures. I found one in ANSOC. His name was Father Courtney Sampson. At our annual ANSOC retreat, after worship, Bible study, strategic planning meetings, meals and evening prayer we would sit around a huge fire outside. We would sing praise songs and share our testimonies, and we all laughed at Linda. He was always the life of the party. He was a theology student at UWC and lived at my father's residence. He was like my big brother.

One night, with the fire still burning bright, my roommate and I decided to walk back to our dorm room. It was pitch dark and all we had was a small torch to light the way. Since our dorm was behind the church building, we knew we had to walk past the graveyard. The gravestones stood silently; we did not dare breathe. Row upon row like soldiers who had long been forgotten, these gravestones were unnerving. A shrill scream shattered the silence and we nearly died! It was Linda! He followed us to make sure that we were safe and got back to our dorm okay. We lightly punched him in the arm because he had frightened us but thanked him for his concern.

Being part of ANSOC was when I felt the strongest sense of community connectivity on campus and most of it was thanks to the leadership and pastoral care provided by Father Courtney Sampson.

According to Erikson's (1968a) psychosocial lifespan theory, developmentally, at this stage I was straddling between young adulthood and middle adulthood. So, the psychosocial modalities I was working through were to find my voice, to find out who I was in relation to my peers, and to deal with intimacy issues such as close friendships, close family members and seriously thinking about romantic relationships. This was a huge stressor for me during this time of my life.

Earlier, during my teenage years, I had no care in the world about friends and romantic relationships. My younger sister was my best friend and my parents prohibited me from dating until I had finished at least my Honours degree. So, until 21 years of age, I could not get my parent's permission or blessing to go on dates. In hindsight, this made me very naïve and inexperienced when it came to relationships in general. It became more apparent that my sheltered upbringing influenced my personality development when I started participating in societies on campus where I was exposed to the diversity of our population. Meeting people from various backgrounds was interesting at this stage of my development. There were key individuals that eased the transition from teenager to adulthood. And Father Courtney Sampson was one of them.

Father Sampson is a wise man and an amazing role model. I first met him when my family attended his church services in Bellville South when I was a teenager. When he became the university's chaplain, he hosted church services and gave theology students opportunities to preach when we congregated as the ANSOC on Sunday mornings.

I could tell Father Sampson anything and he was always there to provide strong scriptural guidance to any problem I faced as a student.

I had a friend who lived in Ruth First, one of the female residences at UWC. She was also an ANSOC member. Driving home from the creepy convent Father Sampson overheard us quarreling in the 16-seater. My friend was angry because I mixed and mingled with everyone at the retreat, and I didn't include her in our discussions or hikes. I apologised but told her that it did not take away from the fact that we were going back home together and that she would always be my friend even when I made new friends. She was not listening to a word I was saying. Father Courtney turned around and faced both of us softly whispering that we needed to see him when we got back home. After his intervention our friendship only grew in strength to her dying day.

The most exciting part of graduation day was the preparation leading up to it. The dress, the shoes, the hair, the make-up, the after-party preparation, everything was so electrifying. My mother's older sister, who was also my godmother, reminded me of Cinderella's fairy godmother because she is an amazing seamstress. She designed and created an exquisite burgundy satin floor-length dress. When I went for my final fitting, she said: "You will look so glamorous with this elegant dress as you make your way across the stage to collect that hard-earned degree, we are all so proud of you." Yes, she teared up, too.

I will never forget my first graduation: Bachelor of Arts, majoring in Psychology and Philosophy. It was 1998, we were the first free psychology majors graduating at UWC because we started our journey in 1995, our first year of liberation from the cataclysmic apartheid tyranny.

I smiled from morning, noon and night when I woke up to the realisation that it was graduation day, knowing that I'd made all my family proud. Graduation day was not only about the ceremony, party, cake, dress, make-up, nails, hair, cap and gown, and the gifts that I received from friends and family; it was about the liberation movement. It was about honouring the legacies of the Hector Pietersens, the lives of the young and old cut short in South Africa's struggle for freedom.

I sat in the bathtub for what seemed like hours, waiting for my mother and close family members who were attending the ceremony. Truth be told, I was soaking up all I had heard and read of the 1976 Soweto march in protest against learning in Afrikaans. I was born in 1976, it was a significant turning point in the country because the revolt was the beginning of the exodus of young people facilitated by the African National Congress and the Pan African Congress. This meant that our youth were sent underground in exile to other countries to keep them safe from the brutality of the apartheid state. By the grace of God, I could walk on that stage and be admitted by the late UWC chancellor, Bishop Desmond Tutu, an Anglican, and a political icon, because of the sacrifices the youth made the year I was born.

I was extremely honoured and felt a huge sense of obligation to continue to make not only my family proud but to contribute to the healing of our nation. One degree at a time.

My mother and aunties' incessant knocking on the bathroom door broke my train of thought as I wiped away my tears of joy and fixed my make-up. I opened the door and stepped into my future with my heart filled with gratitude and hope. Hope that I would do justice to the great sacrifices of black people who had died and survived the political struggle made for my generation and those to come.

I enrolled for an Honours in Psychology with a focus on research and psychometry, and I graduated in 1999. I was awarded Psychology Student of the Year. There was at least one student from each department that was chosen for their contribution to the greater good of the faculty. My parents were invited to a gala dinner hosted by the dean of the faculty of Community and Health Sciences.

Working towards my Honours degree in Psychology was not exclusively about coursework, classes and assessments. It was so much more. We were a fiery group of activists. I was enthusiastically involved in creating mental health literacy campaigns on residence during SWOT week and throughout the year on main campus. My good friend Charl Davids and I, together with a group of like-minded friends in our Honours class, rallied together to establish what we called a Psychology Students Society (PSS). I was the interim chairperson of the PSS and later Charl became the president-elect. We went away on planning retreats; camping, colluding and conjuring up a lifetime of memories that I will always cherish.

When we went camping as a large group of Honours students, we organised and mobilised plans to create strategic mental health literacy campaigning on campus. We, the 1995 cohort of the first *free psychologists* in South Africa, knew our mandate. Looking back now, I see the rose-tinted glasses and minds full of hope that we would lead psychology to establish a new frontier. Inspired by our lecturers, like Professor Cheryl Potgieter, we felt like the world was our oyster.

8

The liberation struggle continues

"So, you really want to become an academic?" asked Kopano Ratele when I proposed my master's by thesis in Psychology idea to him. He had this smirk on his face like he could see my future. My thesis topic was: "The participation of women in rap music: An exploratory study of the role of gender discrimination" (Pretorius, 2001).

I signed up for an MA research internship at a research institute at UWC. At the start of this academic journey, I had not realised, like many other students who register to complete a master's by thesis, that I would not be able to register with the Health Professions Council of South Africa (HPCSA) without doing research coursework. Basically, I was self-taught, and when I did the internship at the institute with students who had completed coursework MAs, I was surprised to learn that they did not already know how to use the basic quantitative analytic tool: the Statistical Package for Social Sciences (SPSS). Most students at historically white universities who study research in psychology are exposed to statistical and qualitative analytic tools in their undergraduate courses or at Honours-level. This is what I find contentious, not only with the discipline of psychology but with the state of higher education in South Africa as a whole. Allow me to explain.

Not all universities were created equal. Apartheid academics made sure of that. The UWC's first council members and professors comprised mainly of white males, ensuring that the Bantu Education System would maintain its influence in higher education. The Bantu Education Act of 1953 was a tool to ensure an unskilled black labour force, and thus to maintain the purpose of apartheid. Tabata, leader of the Non-European Unity Movement, called the policy "education for barbarism" (Tabata, 1960, p. 12). Mamphele Ramphele shared Tabata's view and took it a step further. Even after the Bantu Education Act had long been abolished, she insisted that its remnants were still echoing in the hallways of historically black universities and colleges in South Africa. Then the deputy vice-chancellor of UCT, Ramphele (1999) argued that democratic South Africa's education system was worse than what it was during apartheid, and I have first-hand experience.

When I started my MA internship it should not have come as a surprise to me that five years post-apartheid, psychology students at previously disadvantaged universities still did not have access to the same toolbox as their white counterparts. This has implications for marketing oneself and gaining access to job opportunities. I soon realised that I would have to upskill and be creative in how I applied myself.

The student interns at the institute thought I was privileged because I did not rightfully complain about not receiving our first pay-cheque in January. I had worked at a radio station for three months as a journalist intern and had saved up the money I'd made this way prior to starting the MA research internship. The English Department at UWC piloted a journalism course and I registered for it while I was finishing up my Honours in Psychology. I always juggled more than one thing at a time because I got bored easily and my brain needed constant stimulation.

It was a paid internship at a community radio station. I presented, engineered and produced a health show. This also involved doing edutainment about anti-drug campaigns in high-risk areas around Cape Town as well as raising HIV awareness in schools. Live broadcasts from schools were my favourite. I was in my element producing and presenting multi-media psychoeducational programming. Who knew then that I would end up using these skills I had learnt in broadcast journalism in the lecture room?

He huffed and puffed, our psychology head of department. Walking towards the institute, I ran into him. He said that I was in a lot of trouble! I was confused. It seemed that the interns were not the only ones who had a bone to pick with me. I was called in by the director of the institute and the HOD was there. They wanted to make it clear to me that even though I was doing an internship with student research psychologists registered with the professional board, I was not a student research psychologist because I had not done a coursework master's degree. I could have been cheeky and replied, "But they know just as little as I do; they can hardly create codes for SPSS analysis", but instead I held my tongue. I did not want to upset the HOD even more than I'd apparently already had. They concluded that my job description had to change to research assistant instead of research intern.

At that point in my career development I was so confused, and I felt like someone did not want me to be there. One day, an intern confided in me and told me that the other interns together with our supervising professor were pressurising the director of the institute to get rid of me on the grounds that I was not a registered student research psychologist with the HPCSA. Little did I know that I was caught in the middle of an age-old tug-of-war between professional psychologists and academics.

I felt the tension in different ways, like being excluded from project meetings and being sidelined so that I did not get the chance to upskill. Working at the institute was not professionally challenging any more, and I started to look for a way out.

Dr Bailey, a psychologist and professor at Howard University was introduced to us, the MA students, one day. She was working closely with our supervising professor on a research project. She was interested in my thoughts and ideas, and said that if I wanted to, she would give me a paid internship at Howard University. I was so excited. I had never left the country, nor had I ever gone anywhere far from home without my parents. I was scared but thrilled at the same time.

When I realised that the UWC internship was not working out, I took unpaid leave for three months and left for Washington, DC and Howard University's Center for Drug Abuse Research. At Howard, Dr Bailey exposed me to teaching first years, data collection and analysis on SPSS. I was almost done with my master's and during the three months I worked at Howard University I communicated with my supervisor via mail because Gmail was not then equipped to handle large attachments. After my time at Howard, I returned to South Africa to complete my contract at the institute and to graduate.

My father did not attend my MA graduation because of an argument we had. During my undergraduate and my Honours studies, my father's alcohol use disorder had peaked. This disrupted my learning as he was mostly under the influence of alcohol, and violent during exam times. It got so bad that I had to either spend late nights on main campus, at the general study hall, or sleep over at a friend's place. Working at the university residence and with students you would think that my dad would be more considerate and allow a stress-free study period during SWOT week.

As a substance-use disorder researcher, I now understand that someone with alcohol use disorder does not have an on or off switch to accommodate those around them. My dad was sick, but I did not see that then. All I saw was him being spiteful and selfish. It was during this period that we had a serious argument because I'd asked him not to drink at my graduation and embarrass me.

Most of my extended family members had also lost interest at this point since this was my third degree even though I was in fact the first cousin from both sides of the family to obtain a master's degree. My mother was ashamed of how my father reacted, but she supported me and attended my graduation. It was a bitter-sweet experience.

* * *

I was offered a research associate job at Howard University but had to wait 18 months for my work permit. In the meantime, I was reading and searching for possible PhD projects.

Some female scholars say that graduating with a degree is like giving birth to a new-born. The moment a woman brings a baby into the world you do not dare ask her when she is going to have her next child because pregnancy and birth are so laborious, both physically and emotionally. Yet even though a master's is usually a terminal degree for psychologists, I always knew I wanted to do a PhD in Psychology so when I walked onto the stage to accept my MA in Psychology, I was already thinking about my next adventure.

How could I forget the day I sat at my father's desk and googled experts in alcohol research in South Africa? Charles Parry's name kept coming up and so did his contact details. I picked up the phone and started dialling his office number. After a few rings, a male voice picked up and said: "Charles Parry, how can I help you?" I froze. I started to giggle and said: "Wow, I did not expect you to answer the phone! You are so famous!"

He laughed out loud and thanked me for the compliment but was extremely modest about it. I told him that I had just returned from Howard University where I had worked at the Center for Drug Abuse Research for three months. He knew Dr Bailey. I told him that I was looking for gaps in alcohol research particularly as it pertained to women, and he told me to set up a meeting with his secretary. I was shaking. I never thought that the leading specialist in alcohol research in the country would want to meet with me.

Charles Parry offered me an MA internship at the Alcohol, Drug and Research Group at the Medical Research Council (MRC). There,

I went over their alcohol treatment surveillance data dating back many years and many journal articles pertaining to Charles Parry and his team's research on women and alcohol use disorder search for gaps in the literature. I mainly worked on developing my PhD proposal.

I planned to register for my doctoral degree at Stellenbosch University and to gain ethical clearance while I was working at Howard University. Professor Toni Naidoo and I communicated via email and telephone when I started working on the proposal initially. And Prof. Parry also played a major role in my proposal development. My topic was: "Women's discourse about secretive alcohol dependence and experiences of accessing treatment" (Pretorius, 2010). In fact, my proposal was complete when I resigned from the MRC.

Let's keep count: this was my third MA research "internship"; first at UWC, second at Howard University and a third at the MRC. So, what I lacked in theoretical grounding as a registered research psychologist, I gained through experience by signing up for several internships, learning on the job and contributing to large national and international surveys related to substance use disorder. This was my passion and purpose because it had personal significance, too.

When my work permit was approved and I collected my visa from the embassy, I started planning my trip to Washington. This was my second time leaving home and South Africa. My parents were devastated. My father had always called me his rock. I never understood why because he was such an anchor in my life (when he was not violent and drinking). My mother cried a lot. She would say: "My child, you have nobody there, why must you leave?" Truth be told, I had someone waiting there for me.

9

Love and marriage

Before I left for Washington, DC for the first time, I met Mpho on campus and was smitten by this tall dark African–American man. He was registered as a Computer Science undergraduate, a first-year student, when I was completing my master's internship. By the time I was done, he had dropped out and moved back to DC. He was there while I was waiting for my work permit. He bought calling cards and phoned me on our home landline at odd hours because of the time difference between South Africa and the US East Coast. We were in a long-distance relationship without access to cell phones. By the time I reached Washington, DC we were basically engaged. Well, almost.

It was my father's birthday on 5 March in 2000. I was 23. According to Erikson's (1968a) psychosocial theory, I was right on track to yearn for intimacy and grapple with the virtue of being loved and loving intimately. As per family tradition, we went to a steak restaurant for dinner to celebrate my dad's 47th birthday. I invited Mpho.

What I did not know that day was that Mpho was planning to propose to me in a very peculiar way. We gave my father birthday gifts during supper. My father loved receiving gifts. Mpho gave my father a birthday card and in the card he wrote about his love for me and asked my father to give his blessing for our engagement to be married. My father nearly choked on his food and I could not blame him. It was a rather odd and antiquated way to ask for my hand, I thought. But my mother and sisters were so excited and happy for me that I quickly brushed those thoughts aside. Two weeks after my father's birthday, Mpho left South Africa for the United States.

On the 20-something hour-long plane trip to Washington I was fuelled by excitement, as I imagined what living there for the at least three-year duration of my work permit would be like. Mpho was waiting for me at the airport, and I was so excited to see him hold up a "Welcome home" banner.

I arrived over the weekend so that I could rest and shake off the jet lag before my first day at work on the following Monday. I was employed as a research assistant to the director of the Center for Drug Abuse Research, housed in the Psychology Department at Howard University.

Working at another historically black institution like Howard University made me feel like I was part of a black consciousness movement. Even though there were no protests like at UWC, students and faculty were constantly in public dialogue about the state of the nation. Was Howard University a politically charged campus? Yes. Did this excite me? Yes. I felt right at home.

I was mesmerised by Howard University because it was pre-dominately black, with state-of-the-art resources. This was refreshing and saddening at the same time. It made me sad because I did not want to have to leave my country to gain specialised academic experience.

I was 26 when we got married. I already had my master's degree. After I completed the proposal and ethics clearance was granted, I registered for the doctoral programme at Stellenbosch University. But I could not work on my thesis and I'm ashamed to admit why.

Mpho did not have a degree and was working as a project administrator in a property development firm. By the time we got married, he was adamant about my not getting a doctoral degree before he graduated with his Associate Bachelor's from a community college. He said that I would make him look bad. A woman is not supposed to be more qualified than her husband!

Ironically, it was the same reason why my father was against our relationship. My father thought that I should marry a doctor or at least a professor. Nonetheless, both my parents attended our wedding. It was the first time they had left South Africa.

"Liezille, the limo's here, oh my word, we are driving in a limo. Get dressed, Liezille. You cannot leave this man at the altar. Liezille what about the limo?" exclaimed my excited and elated mother. But I was downcast and not really ready to get married.

A month before the wedding I called friends from a pay-phone outside the apartment and asked them for advice. I had no family but a few very close friends who felt like family in DC. As I prepared to walk down the aisle, I realised that I didn't actually see a future with Mpho. How was I going to start, let alone finish, my PhD under a cloud of such uncertainty?

Mpho found out that I was having doubts about going through with the wedding and so he called me. He said everything would be different when we got married. Things would change. I was hopeful, gullible and felt pressured by my parents to save them the embarrassment as my *lobola* (bride-price) had literally been the price of their plane tickets.

If I were to strictly follow Erikson's theory of psychosocial development, in hindsight, I would have preferred isolation in place of intimacy if it meant my PhD in psychology was at stake. This is where I disagree with Erikson's theory. I was inexperienced with relationships at the time I met Mpho. I was 23 years old when he proposed. What did I know about love and commitment other than what I saw in movies or read in fairy tales as a child? At 25 years old I was not ready to get married to a man who, not only did not support my career, but didn't support it because he felt threatened by my ambition. Why does Erikson's theory and society (people like my parents) make you choose between a marriage (intimacy) or a career (isolation)? I had no business making such a life-changing decision when my brain had not even fully developed (according to neuro-psychologists).

Nothing changed when we were married. I secretly emailed my father from my work computer at the university and sent him my registration form. He enrolled me as a PhD student at Stellenbosch University. I tried working on the literature and theoretical chapters in the first year of my marriage but did not get far. I had to stop because we had planned that I would fall pregnant two years after we got married. I was so young and so naïve.

I was 27 going on 28. The phone rang, it was after 6:00 pm on a Wednesday evening. "Hello, is this Lee?" Most Americans could not pronounce my full name, so going by "Lee" made it easier for them. It was my primary care physician. She said I was pregnant and that she had made an appointment for me with an OBGYN and wanted to check if I was available. Mpho was in the kitchen and I screamed: "I'm pregnant!"

He was so shocked he did not even make eye contact. I touched his arm to get his attention, looked him dead in the eyes and said: "I'm pregnant, as we planned!" He pulled away and was downcast – he was acting strangely. He acted as if we had not planned for this to happen. He behaved as if he was not sitting next to me in the doctor's office a day ago excited because my period was late. I retired to my room and did not speak a word of it until the next day when I got home from work.

He was home early which was unusual. "I resigned from my job today," he said. In horror I screamed: "Why would you do that without talking to me about it first? Babies cost money you know?" He said that he needed a higher paying job. My parents had always advised that it was not wise to leave a job unless you had something else lined up. I was devastated. I went to work every day and he just watched TV and ate all the food in the house.

The house was always a mess when I got home from work. Most days I contemplated suicide. Jumping in front of an oncoming train would be far better than being a single parent, I thought. I was lonely and I could not share what I was experiencing with anyone because I was just too ashamed.

This experience taught me an enormous life lesson. Something about Erikson's first stage of psychosocial stage development, that is, that trust versus mistrust stirs up sadness. The significant relationship during this developmental stage is the one you have with your mother. Hope and faith are the virtues that this stage's psychosocial modality for healthy personality development promises. My mom had been a stay-at-home mom and she told me that she had breastfed me until I was about 18 months old. We developed a strong bond throughout my life. Both my parents always made good on their promises and this instilled hope and faith in me which translated into my trusting people implicitly. Of course, with the hope that they meant everything they said and with faith that everything would go according to plan. Mpho taught me differently. And this was my entry into motherhood. Alone, isolated and in a foreign country, married, pregnant, with a husband who could not be trusted.

On a cold, unusually snowy day in 2004, my daughter was born. I had to have a c-section because she was breached. I was in a lot of pain. Mpho slept over at the hospital with me and our baby because I had a private ward.

I never felt so alone. I would cry from the debilitating pain I was in and he would kick my bed in anger because I was complaining, causing more pain. I was either disturbing his sleep or he was too proud to ask the nurses to attend to me.

My friends brought me flowers and that cheered me up. I loved how they fussed over my baby and wanted to make sure I was okay.

She was the sweetest baby ever. She would never cry. She was so even-tempered that I considered resuming my PhD at Stellenbosch University. I had my own laptop and Mpho started taking on temporary shift work (he still did not have a decent job, nor had he made any progress towards finishing his Associate Bachelor's). He would never find out that I had resumed my studies, right? Wrong.

One day he found my laptop open on the bed next to me when he came home from his shift. I was asleep. He saw that I had been writing again. I will never forget that night. Baby was asleep in her crib because I was still recovering from the c-section. I was awakened by a choking feeling, as if I was suffocating. I opened my eyes to Mpho strangling me. I saw death in his eyes! Baby must have sensed evil in the room because she started screaming, which she never did. He immediately loosened his grip, grabbed my laptop, and stomped on it repeatedly, ensuring that it was irreparable. With each stomp I felt like he was killing a piece of me locked up in the hard drive of that laptop.

This was the beginning of our end. He said: "This is your fault! Look what you did! Make that baby quiet!" I was crying uncontrollably and was of no use to my baby at that moment. "I told you not to pursue that PhD. Why can't you be a good supportive woman?" he said. I had two more months left of maternity leave, but I had to get back to work sooner because I was dying inside.

When I returned to work, I renewed my contract and got another three-year work permit as a research associate at the Howard University Hospital (HUH), Health Disparities in the Pediatrics Department working on biopsychosocial-related research projects. I really enjoyed this position because I was able to gain more analytical research skills and wrote my first couple of scientific publications. Things were going so well that the director allowed me to go and work on some of her projects in South Africa. This granted me the opportunity to introduce my baby to the family and to start the registration process at Stellenbosch University to collect data. The plan was for me to collect my data at home and return to the US to analyse and finish the thesis with constant feedback from my supervisor. That was the plan, but Mpho made sure that it would not come to fruition.

I was planning a trip home, but it was as if the powers that be did not want me to leave Washington Dulles Airport. We were already seated and ready for the first SAA direct flight from Washington, DC to Cape Town. We were disembarked twice. The engine caught fire and other technical difficulties delayed us a second time. We were put up in airport accommodation until the next plane came from Cape Town. This took two days. Mpho was so worried and scared that he joined us and slept over in the hotel because he was overwhelmed that he could have lost us if the plane crashed. It was a very emotionally intense time for us, and I felt so safe and secure when he was with our baby and me. I believe that was when baby number two, our son, was conceived.

My daughter and I landed in Cape Town and were greeted by my parents and younger sister.

They were so excited to meet my little American baby. It took her a while to get used to everyone. One day, after being home for about two weeks, Mpho called and said: "Pick me up from the airport." I was confused. He said he could not live without us for three months, so he gave up our apartment. Left all our things to be sold and moved back to South Africa so that I could support his studies. I was hysterical. Again, no consultation. No plan. No regard for the position I held at HUH. I was 29 years old.

I did not know how to break the news to my director. I could not go back to DC because I did not have a place to stay with my baby. I did not, I could not, burden any of my friends with my problems. I felt awful but I had to resign.

Fortunately, for my baby's sake, I immediately got a job at the University of Cape Town's psychiatry department under the leadership of the late Prof. Alan Flischer. I enjoyed the work I did with

Alan. We conducted a process evaluation of the LoveLife programme in various schools in the Western and Southern Cape. I got this job because of the HIV/Aids-related experience I had gained at Howard University and the work I did as an Honours student. This position required me to stay in the Southern Cape (Knysna and George) for three months to collect data. When the UCT research associate position came to an end I was ready to start working on my PhD.

10

Becoming a doctor

I met the renowned Professors Mbewu and Reddy at a dinner party when they were in Washington, DC. They said if I ever came back to South Africa to finish my PhD, I should sign up for a PhD internship with Prof. Reddy in the Health Promotion, Research and Development Unit at the South African Medical Research Council (SAMRC).

Prof. Reddy welcomed me with open arms, and I was able to finish my PhD in two and a half years. That is how much support I received from Prof. Reddy and the SAMRC. My internship paid for my registration fees; Prof. Reddy gave me access to her car to collect data; she wrote letters of support to allow me to work during December holidays when the Council was closed because I did not own my own laptop and I did not have access to the internet; I worked on nothing else but my PhD.

Mpho found out again. He went through my phone and saw text messages between me and my supervisor. I can still taste the blood in my mouth just reflecting on this moment in my life. I woke up because of a pounding headache. He was standing over the bed with my canon camera in his hand. He had smashed the right side of my temple with it and that is what woke me. He dragged me by my hair (I have a thick bush of curly hair), and he started hitting me and screaming at me. I was mortified. I was inconsolable. He took down the professor's number and said he would call him later to cancel our meetings. He stomped on my phone and broke it.

When I got to the office my sweet friend could see that I was hurting. She took me into her office and consoled me. At lunch-time she took me to the mall and bought me my first Blackberry. I, of course, paid her off monthly until we were squared. She was an angel. She had bailed me out of predicaments with Mpho so many times. He would come to my office looking for trouble and she would block him without my even knowing.

She encouraged me to get an interdict against him. It was during the 16 days of activism, a gender-based violence campaign to raise awareness and intervention on violence against women and girls. The police contacted me every year after that incident to check on me. I appreciated that. It was not a pleasant annual reminder, but it was a memory that ignited survival against all odds. In fact, the police department checking on me for years after I reported the incident was also a hallmark of my determination to succeed in following my heart and obtaining a PhD. I was the first on my mother's side of the family to ever accomplish such an achievement and I give God all the glory. You might not understand the biblical reference here, but because I am a Christian, I know that this was the only way I was able to survive all the roadblocks to obtaining my PhD. All the angels that were sent my way to assist me in graduating are too countless to mention but they know who they are, and I will never let them forget how grateful I am. A year before I graduated, Mpho emailed me and said the divorce was final. I did not believe him, so I asked a friend in DC to double-check. I was so relieved. Free at last! My luck was turning.

Even though I was free from misogynistic jealousy, I still had two small children who needed a mother and a father. So, I had to take on multiple roles. I was a juggler. Looking back, I still remember my struggles to finish my doctorate vividly. I would wake up at four in the morning. I would put the kids in their car seats while they were sleeping and take them to the car one by one. Of course, I had to hurry in case one of them woke up and did not see me. Luckily, they always slept right through. I would then drive to my parents' house to use my father's computer and internet connection to work on my thesis for at least three hours. Then the school run, then off to work. I would pick the kids up from day care at five in the afternoon, drive to my parents, hand them over to my mom and get back in front of my dad's computer. I would stop to eat supper with my parents and the kids, wash them and put them in their car seats so that it would be easier to carry them to the car when I left my parents' house. I used to work until after eleven at night. I usually got home around midnight.

* * *

Growing up on the Cape Flats and in the rural Ciskei where there are little to no recreational activities for youth, I experienced first-hand how easy it was to participate in risky behaviour. Working at the Health Promotion and Research Development Unit at the SAMRC I was given an opportunity to collect data and coordinate a few provinces as part of a national study.

The second Youth Risk Behaviour Survey (YRBS) was a national study undertaken in South Africa to establish the prevalence of key risk behaviours, namely: intentional and unintentional injuries, violence and traffic safety, suicide-related behaviours, behaviours related to substance abuse (tobacco, alcohol and other drugs), sexual behaviour, nutrition and dietary behaviours, physical activity and hygiene-related behaviours (Amosun et al., 2007). Professor Reddy, who was the head of the Health Promotion and Research

Development Unit at the South African Medical Research Council, was commissioned by South Africa's national Department of Health to undertake the Youth Risk Behaviour Survey. It consisted of sampling 23 schools per province, from which 14 766 learners were sampled, 10 699 of whom participated. The terms of reference were to provide nationally and provincially representative data on the prevalence of the above behaviours that place school-going learners at risk.

Being part of this major study was eye-opening. I was in awe of how meticulously Professor Reddy managed this large-scale study. She was very dedicated to the project. When it came to preparation for data collection, she would stay at the office with us until 3:00 in the morning making sure that the boxes were packed and all the necessary research apparatus had been methodically packaged and was ready to be shipped off to each province.

This was an unforgettable experience. Even though my main purpose was to complete my doctoral thesis, I really wanted to participate in SAYRBS because it was ground-breaking research. Of particular interest to me was the prevalence of alcohol consumption of South African youth over the years, as depicted in the table below.

Table 1. South African adolescents' alcohol consumption by gender: Findings from the Youth Risk Behaviour Survey

Alcohol consumption	2002		2008		2011	
	Male	Female	Male	Female	Male	Female
Ever used alcohol, %	56.1	43.5	54.4	45.1	53.8	44.9
Current alcohol use (past 30 days), %	38.5	26.4	40.5	29.5	36.6	28.2
Binge drinking past month, %	29.3	17.9	33.3	23.7	30.3	20.1
Age of initiation <13years, %	15.8	9.0	15.3	8.6	16.3	8.7

During my PhD internship I submitted an abstract to attend the annual National Institute of Drug Authority's (NIDA) international conference held in Nevada. I applied for a travel grant and was awarded the Commonwealth Prize together with a director of the China Center for Disease Control in Wuhan. He and I were awarded USD 5 000 and a research fellowship with a NIDA-funded researcher. I got to spend my research fellowship at Johns Hopkins University Hospital's substance use disorder treatment facility. It was a rich experience that I'll always cherish. I learnt the harm of a reductionist biopsychosocial approach to understanding the complexities of drug use, abuse and addiction. I learnt that women who are pregnant and use illegal substances are frustrated because their pregancies alone are not enough incentive to stop them from using. While I agree that it is hard to modify behaviour on a whim, I recognise that the unborn child is placed at immense risk and is born with irreversible birth defects.

My fellow winner of the NIDA Commonwealth Prize for research spent his fellowship at Yale University. We had dinner together the last night of the conference and we vowed to keep in touch. He went as far as inviting me to Wuhan on a fact-finding mission on the ways we could conduct collaborative studies since our interests were similar. He also wanted to bring a delegation to South Africa so that he could understand what issues we were grappling with. I was excited for our future collaborations but, alas, I still needed to complete my PhD.

The SAMRC has an annual conference for its interns to showcase their work and to give postgraduate students exposure to presenting their research. My thesis was in its final stages, so I presented my work. This was not the first conference I had presented at. When I worked in Washington I had presented at several tri-state conferences. I loved presenting my work. I gained exceptional skills from the community psychology Honours course I took with Professor Cheryl Potgieter. Yet I was very surprised to win the best PhD presentation in my category. I still have the diploma. I also received ZAR 20 000 in cash for the best PhD conference presentation.

Final submission day dawned. My oral examination date was set. I knew who my examiners were because they were the most cited alcohol-related researchers in South Africa and abroad. I worked with Charles Parry before and Curdore Snell was my international examiner who I had the pleasure to meet and work with while I was in Washington. Still, I was a ball of nerves. I studied my thesis back to front a thousand times.

On cloud nine. Butterflies. Honoured. Exhilarated. Emotional. I cannot come up with enough words to describe how I felt on 10 December 2010. For so many years, a PhD in Psychology had seemed unobtainable because of the harsh reality stacked up against me: misogynistic punishment for wanting to further my education.

My graduation was the first and most probably the last family photograph we took. My father never liked to have his picture taken. This is evident in my graduation pictures. If it were not true, it would be funny. I can still hear my father's voice and cadence in my head when I recall his impatience with all the pictures we took.

I wanted to document this momentous occasion. My mom, my sisters and I all wore black dresses (this was not planned). My family portrait symbolises the synchronicity of souls coming together as one to honour the sacrifices my parents made to make sure that we had a bright future. I am deeply grateful for the opportunity I was given to complete my doctorate in psychology at Stellenbosch University.

When I entered the graduation hall, all the graduates cloaked in black gowns were already seated. We walked in with our red gowns and everyone cheered. While I was seated, I glanced over the crowd to see if I could catch a glimpse of my family. My parents and siblings were seated quite close to where I was. I teared up immediately when I saw them. Before the proceedings started, I ran over to them, gave them a hug and we shed happy tears.

It is difficult to describe in words how I felt on my graduation day. There is a sense of uniqueness when you graduate from a previously whites-only university. The clock stopped. Hundreds of eyes peering at you when your name is called, and your supervisor reads your abstract. I felt like I was standing on that stage for an eternity. I felt a bit out of place amongst my fellow doctoral graduates because I was the only black woman. However, ironically, I graduated with my high school teacher. He also received a PhD at Stellenbosch University on the same day as me. What an amazing experience.

After graduation I took a picture with my high school teacher and my thesis director, Professor Toni Naidoo.

My high school teacher, Yule Davids, told me that he was starting a postdoctoral fellowship at the Human Sciences Research Council (HSRC) in January. This came as a surprise. It just so happened that he and I had not only graduated at the same time, but that I would be completing a postdoctoral fellowship at the HSRC, in the same unit, in adjoining offices, with my former high school teacher. I was thrilled that our paths had crossed again, twenty-odd years later.

This was the beginning of a new season in my life. It was remarkable to be in the presence of someone I looked up to as a teacher, this time as his equal, not his pupil. What were the odds?

11

Four times a postdoc

Truth Coffee. That is what I remember having before going up in the lift to the Population Health, Health Systems, and Innovation (PHHS) Unit at the Human Sciences Research Council (HSRC). I took a deep breath and told myself: "No more waiting to become, it is time to be. No more waiting to become, it is time to be." That was my mantra for the entire month.

After my first postdoc at PHHS I felt that I needed additional training in various research methods, so I applied for the South African Research Chairs Initiative (SARChI) in Health and Health Systems, a research postdoc at the School of Public Health, UWC. My cup was running over at this point. Even though the postdoc was only one year, it felt like a three-year programme because it was so labour intensive, but in a good way. I wanted to transition back into public mental health since I had learnt so much about it, and I wanted to shift focus. Social work always fascinated me, so I decided to sign up for another National Research Foundation funded postdoc. I took a bit of a break from higher education to work at the SAMRC but returned after 18 months when I immigrated to Belgium to work at the University of Antwerpen (UA). This was my final postdoc.

But why four postdocs in public mental health? Let me explain.

My first day as a postdoc at PHHS was uneventful because during the first week of January academics are usually still on holiday. However, the junior staff were the welcoming committee. All of them were black people and I felt as if they had wanted to warn me about something sinister, but without the effect of clouding my judgement on my first day. Nonetheless, I was very optimistic about being an academic and continuing with my research in a public mental health space.

The executive director was a retired Greek professor who had a very friendly and welcoming disposition. He was generally very supportive of my work and encouraged me to look for funding opportunities to grow my research portfolio. He had very strict performance targets set for me. I had to publish at least two articles in accredited journals, develop at least one funding proposal, attend an international and a local conference, build international and local strategic partnerships, sign memorandums of understanding (MOUs), and the list goes on.

During my three-year postdoctoral fellowship, I gained invaluable experiences. I learnt how to build international partnerships during my PhD internship at the SAMRC. One experience which stands out was the invitation I received from the Wuhan Center for Disease Control (CDC) in China. I visited Wuhan for a month to learn more about the substance use disorder research and interventions they conducted with sex workers.

My time in China was filled with tours of health facilities, meetings with health officials and tourist activities.

Wuhan is a unique city. When I arrived in Wuhan, I was picked up from the airport by my colleague. I last saw Chang in America when we had dinner on the last day of the NIDA conference. He gave me the itinerary and told me that I would be accompanied by a translator daily. When I entered my hotel room, I was shocked to see the bouquet of condoms and sex toys on the dresser. I wondered if it was a gift or standard hotel practice. Nonetheless, I shrugged it off because after all I was coming to find out more about Chinese culture, particularly as it pertained to their substance use consumption trends.

The next day at breakfast I was stunned. Dumplings and noodles for breakfast? The food was the most challenging experience for me. I ate papaya and frog spawn. I learnt that one does not refuse to eat anything that Chinese people offer you as it is a great insult to them. This was a big challenge for me because I am a very fussy eater. At breakfast that morning, I settled for coffee before running downstairs to meet my chaperon.

I asked her about the condoms in my bedroom. We chuckled and she concluded that it is not standard practice and had no idea who left them in my room.

The first meeting was basically an introduction to the Wuhan Center for Disease Control's senior staff, and I gave a presentation on the South African healthcare system and how substance use disorder is treated in the public healthcare system.

The most fascinating discovery was the CDC's ability to profile sex workers and their substance use. Sex work is huge in Wuhan, central Hubei province. In fact, I will go as far to say that sex workers are more popular than karaoke bars in Wuhan. This is prevalent in hair salons, hotels, of course, and massage parlours. It was not advisable for me to actively seek out the sex workers who formed part of an intervention group the Wuhan CDC was implementing. Yet, I was fortunate to visit the medical facilities that administered methadone to sex workers who also happen to be on antiretroviral therapy (ART). As part of my fact-finding mission, I visited a few brothels, noticed that they were not cheap, and the clients were quite affluent. One of the interventions run by the CDC in collaboration with women's rights NGOs was distributing condoms and Aids-prevention pamphlets to brothels in Wuhan.

As popular as sex work was in Wuhan, sex workers faced grave discrimination and worked closely with NGOs to decrimilalise their trade. I was told that sex workers are afraid of using condoms because of the threats they face when they do. So, most sex workers numb the pain of undermining their preferences of practising safe sex by using illegal substances such as heroin.

When I returned to South Africa my priority was to contact the Sex Workers Education and Advocacy Trust (SWEAT). I met with the resident psychologist. She invited me to join their weekly meeting with sex workers. I wanted to profile sex workers to develop an intervention in collaboration with my Wuhan colleague.

What I learnt from this experience was never to judge people by their actions but to understand what lies beneath. Most of the sex workers I interviewed were males. They were either men sleeping with men or transgender (males transitioning to be female). I was not allowed to interview them where they worked and so SWEAT provided a venue where I was able to observe the psychologist and nurse implement life skills orientation such as basic hygiene (bathing after each sexual encounter).

Working at the HSRC as a postdoctoral fellow opened up many pioneering experiences such as working on the first ever South African National Health and Nutrition Examination Survey (SANHANES). This major national survey was conducted in each province. This study was supported by several national governmental departments as well as international organisations. The rationale for this study was that even though communicable diseases such as HIV and TB were a high priority, increasingly non-communicable diseases such as heart disease, cancer and diabetes were becoming a leading threat to the health and development of the human species. SANHANES set out to determine to what extent risk factors, such as tobacco use, unhealthy diet, physical inactivity, and the harmful use of alcohol could be prevented. The focus of the SANHANES project was to prevent the mortality and disease burden with which these health problems confronted our country.

I worked with a team of research specialists who were interested in the rate of alcohol consumption nationally. Geographically, we found that Mpumalanga reported the highest alcohol consumption and in terms of race, white men reported a significantly higher level of problem drinking in the country. These results affected me on a personal level as someone who had been labelled as a coloured during the apartheid era. The stereotype that coloured people were heavy drinkers was exposed as a myth that was dispelled by the SANHANES study.

Before I left the HSRC I collaborated with a professor in journalism from Howard University. We conducted two studies entitled: "The construction of femininity, race and sexuality in alcohol advertisements in South African and American women's magazines" (Jacobs & Tyree, 2013) and "Can you save me? Black male superheroes in Hollywood film" (Tyree & Jacobs, 2014). To this day we've never met in person.

The most exciting role I played at the HSRC was being nominated by the national Department of Health as chairperson of the food-based dietary guidelines alcohol advisory task team. Our task team was commissioned to conduct research on how much alcohol was safe to consume by the South African nation. Charles Parry had been the previous chairperson of the food-based dietary guideline. Needless to say, I was very honoured by this appointment. One of the deliverables was to produce an accredited journal article. I co-published with the renowned nutrition scientist in the country, Professor Nelia Steyn. Our article was entitled "'If you drink alcohol, drink sensibly.' Is this guideline still appropriate?" (Jacobs & Steyn, 2013).

Exciting things were happening in my life after my PhD graduation. While I was working as a postdoctoral researcher at the HSRC, I remarried and had a little girl, my third and last born.

My husband is the total opposite of my first love. We've had our problems like most couples, but nothing could prepare me for the loving kindness and support I get from him.

One day my husband, baby and I were driving from work after we had picked her up from his parents in Manenberg. His mom looked after our baby when I returned to work. We had stopped at a red traffic light when we were rear-ended by the car behind us. We were caught in a four-car pile-up. Instinctively, when we were hit, I flung my left hand out in front of my baby who was seated next to me in the back of the car. Thankfully, she was securely strapped into her car seat and did not even cry after impact. I wasn't as lucky. I was seriously injured. I could not move my legs and my lower back felt numb with pain.

After the police left the scene, my husband, who was uninjured, drove us to the nearest emergency room. Thankfully I did not fracture any bones but had major muscle spasm. After months of physical therapy without the pain improving, my doctor referred me to a rheumatologist. A very eccentric specialist treated me and diagnosed me with fibromyalgia. I remember my husband's delight. "Finally, we have a diagnosis," he exclaimed. But I was more depressed than ever before. With the diagnosis came the harsh reality: there's no cause or cure for fibromyalgia. What's so good about that? Treatment was a trial and error of different opioids.

I gain and lose weight based on what drugs I'm on. Yet the drugs prescribed have not been the worst part of my diagnosis. Whenever I get a cold or any infection, my fibromyalgia tends to flare up for as long as two weeks at a time. When I explain my symptoms to friends and family, they ask me the same questions: "How do you live like this? You are in constant pain, you get sick so easily, you have brain fog, how do you manage to be so high-functioning? Should you not be medically boarded?"

In the US, fibromyalgia is considered a disability and I can see why. I became a fibro-warrior. Hard work and mental resilience are what kept me focused on my career and accepting that I would have to find some kind of quality of life, a willingness to live by setting career goals.

While it was clear that I had my hands full at the HSRC, I did not feel as if I was being challenged enough. I needed to learn more, develop more. So, I was appointed part-time as the chief operations officer (COO) at the South African Monitoring and Evaluation Association (SAMEA).

My role as a senior executive was tasked with overseeing the day-to-day administrative and operational functions of this non-profit organisation. As the COO, I typically reported directly to the board who consisted mostly of high-ranking government officials from the Department of Monitoring and Evaluation (DPME) in the Presidency.

This position required me to show strong leadership, strategic thinking and creative skills, to be results driven and adept at financial management. I needed to develop these skills in order to excel in my capacity as a social scientist. In addition to harnessing all these skills and networking with the top evaluation researchers in the country, I implemented an Evaluation Café. This was a collaboration between SAMEA and the HSRC. Not many HSRC scientists were conducting evaluation research. SAMEA had members all over the country. The HSRC has satellite offices in most provinces. So, I was able to convince the HSRC to link up with SAMEA members nationally for the Evaluation Café once a month during lunch-time. SAMEA members would have the platform to present their research and it was an educational experience for HSRC staff.

Towards the end of my postdoctoral fellowship I was head-hunted by the national Department of Basic Education's research head to work as a director in the research division. The job was running the substance use prevention interventions in primary and high schools, nationally. I opted to work as a postdoctoral fellow at the School of Public Health at UWC instead. The position was to work with a Flemish professor appointed as the South African Research Chairs Initiative (SARChI) in Health and Health Systems research.

Nostalgia. That is what I felt when I started the second postdoctoral fellowship at UWC's School of Public Health (SoPH). Nothing really changed on campus. Walking around my old stomping grounds brought back fond memories of my student life. Yet, this time things were different.

I remember being very enthusiastic about starting this position. Since my previous postdoc had also been in health systems, I was eager to broaden my experience of public mental health issues and health policy. In one year, I got the opportunity to teach research methods to master's in Public Health students. I supervised a master's student to completion and published more articles based on my doctoral thesis. The most noteworthy experience during my postdoc at UWC was managing the Emerging Voices for Global Health (EV4GH) project. It is an advanced, blended learning, training programme for young, promising and emerging health policy and health systems researchers.

The cohort I worked with were mostly recent graduates, medical doctors, decision-makers and other health system role-players with an interest in becoming influential global health voices and local change makers. My role was to coach EV4GH to participate actively in international conferences where global health issues are addressed, and to raise their voices in scientific and policy debates. I worked as part of an internationally representative committee consisting of EV4GH alumni elected by previous EV4GH participants and several invited (liaison) members from EV4GH partner institutes.

My role as project manager and facilitator required me to attend think tanks at the Institute for Tropical Medicine (ITM) in Belgium. The first time I went to Belgium was overwhelming. My colleagues in Belgium were very meticulous, operating at a more urgent pace compared to my South African colleagues; and sometimes demonstrating higher levels of impatience, associating their self-worth with achievement. Their assiduous work ethic was contagious. The skills I learnt from my Belgian colleagues were endless.

E-coaching and distance learning training methods are skills I still apply to this day. Training medical doctors, psychologists, nurses and allied health practitioners in scientific presentation, networking, innovative communication formats was part of my deliverables as a project manager for the EV4GH.

Field visits to local health facilities in Cape Town were also part of the EV4GH programme. Even today, I do field visits with my third-year Critical Health Psychology students. This experience significantly influenced how I make my pedagogy visible to my students.

I also had administrative responsibilities such as coordinating the international public health doctoral programme. This was emotionally draining. Students were scattered all over the world, and many of them lacked motivation and needed daily encouragement. This is where my doctoral experience really served me well. I spent my mornings telling my story to single mothers who lacked the motivation to finish their PhDs because of all the odds stacked against them.

Besides coordinating the doctoral programme, I was also responsible for implementing face-to-face workshops at least once a term. Students would present the status of their doctoral research and workshop on the way forward. This was very useful and inspiring to the students. The fellowship lasted 12 months but I still felt like I needed more training in various research topics and methods related to my research interests. I was offered a third postdoctoral fellowship at UWC's Department of Social Work.

Psychologists rarely consider working in the Department of Social Work. It has been said that social workers are hard-edged, cold and bureaucratic. There is this popular misconception that social workers are only going to abduct your kids and that they are going to put up barriers so that you never regain custody of your child. I experienced nothing but warmth, care and compassion during my time at UWC's social work department.

I taught research methods to undergraduates and postgraduates. The work I enjoyed most was with the head of department, Professor Catherina Schenck. I accompanied her on field visits to landfill sites. Her research was on waste pickers who make a living from anything dumped on landfill sites. While she was collecting data, I would talk to some of the people living on these landfill sites, observing their ways of life. They created makeshift homes out of recycled materials and most of their children were born there and did not attend school. Substance abuse was rampant. Therein lay my interest. Professor Schenck often took her final-year students to landfill sites which I thought was amazing. Students gained hands-on research experience and exposure to what the scope of practice would require of them.

In my opinion, I learnt more about research in practice in the social work department than I did in any other capacity. I supervised fourth-year social work students' research projects on hookah-pipe smoking in families, and published a paper on it, co-wrote a chapter in a parenting book, and supervised two master's students' theses to completion.

My postdoc at the Department of Social Work was short-lived because I had learnt all that I could, and it was time for me to move on. I left the department and took up a position at another science council. Here I would work with research and counselling psychologists as a senior scientist.

Everybody seems to be fighting for a seat at the table at the science councils. I really did not care for the proverbial coveted seat – what concerned me was what was being done under the table. I was employed as a senior scientist, yet I was seated in an open plan office with the research psychology interns, while all other senior staff had their own offices. Most of these interns were privileged white UCT students who owned their own horses and took lavish vacations in London to visit family. The UWC students who interned there were not given a seat at the table. As a senior staff member, I was tasked to conduct literature reviews because the UCT interns were deemed intellectually more capable of engaging in high-level thought processes.

One day while we were planning an international conference, the head of the unit instructed the interns, including me, a senior staff member, to do a practice run of our conference presentations. First, I was offended that I needed to do a practice run for a small conferences (fewer than 100 participants). I had presented papers at large international conferences for many years. I had even trained international doctors on how to present at large international conferences. Yet, I was treated as an intern who had never presented a paper at a conference before.

I was humiliated. At this point I had lived long enough to have had a few chapters I wished I could erase. And a few stories I wished I could rewrite. We all do, right? It is called regret. Yet, knowing the executive director's true character, the decision that led to my greatest regret, working with him, could have been avoided. I could have avoided this experience had I known that I would be entering a time machine, transporting me back to 1953 when the Bantu Education Act was promulgated. This apartheid law intended for black people to be trained for manual, menial labour (like asking someone with a PhD to work exclusively on desktop literature searches). The Minister of Native Affairs, Hendrik Verwoerd, rationalised the apartheid government's education policy to the South African Parliament:

> There is no space for the "Native" in the European Community above certain forms of labour. For this reason it is of no avail for him to receive training which has its aim in the absorption of the European Community, where he cannot be absorbed. Until now he has been subjected to a school system which drew him away from his community and misled him by showing him the greener pastures of European Society where he is not allowed to graze. (Kallaway, 2002)

During the 1950s, black teachers and parents vehemently contested the creation of a separate and unequal education system for black children rather than a single public schooling system for all South Africans (Kallaway, 2002).

If only I had paused to ask myself: "Does working with black people who profess to disrupt social injustice in public but, behind closed doors, degrade, demoralise and destroy the confidence of an up-and-coming female social scientist really harness my potential?"

The executive director singled me out and I felt like he must have been misinformed about me. After my presentation he asked to meet with me. My line manager was present too. I was told that I should be ashamed of my performance. UCT interns were better equipped to conduct a Power Point presentation on their work than I was. This Indian professor insisted that my Bantu Education had set me up for failure and it was time to break away from the shackles of apartheid. The way I interpreted the professor's claims was that subconsciously he agreed with Verwoerd, that black people should be subservient to white people (in this case, white interns from UCT).

I believe that I experienced systemic discrimination while working as a senior scientist at a research council. Systemic discrimination in educational, cultural and social terms has been defined as attitudes by design or impact that affect the limit of a person's right to opportunities because of attributed rather than actual characteristics (Seekings, 2008). I interpret my experience with the executive director as such because, based on his attribution of my background, he assumed that I was trained to function at the lowest cognitive level compared with the UCT-trained students.

He said that he was thinking of demoting me. I was shocked. Angry even. My line manager had called me into his office several times to commend me for exceeding my performance targets and commented on my exceptional work ethic. My line manager and I had a very good work relationship. So, yes, I was shocked and confused about the executive director's blatant bullying and verbally violent disrespect for my professional integrity.

After many insults and violent psychological attacks I finally broke down. I went to my office, closed my door, and cried a river. I could not believe that a black person could be so antagonistic towards me. How could he intentionally destroy my self-esteem and then climb on his soapbox talking about disrupting social injustice. As I said before, I never wanted a seat at their table. I was more interested in what was handed to people like him – in this case an Indian female – under the table. She graduated with her PhD more than 10 years after I did and was immediately promoted to full professorship. This appointment was made because the executive director held a very influential position at a national university.

The concept of employment is complex, encompassing not only a simple labour-for-money exchange but also providing individuals with identity, community and meaning. This is particularly significant for those with disabilities, for whom work can be a source of identity, normality and socialisation (Saunders & Nedelec, 2014).

The distinction between work and job meaning further emphasises the multifaceted nature of employment, with work meaning being influenced by social frameworks and job meaning by situational and personal relevance. However, the issue of informal economic activity, such as "under the table" jobs, complicates this understanding, as it can both draw individuals into the wider economy and challenge assumptions about the "underclass", especially in post-apartheid South Africa (Leonard, 1998).

I mention this now because it relates to my experience with the academe within a discipline laced with injustice and nepotism. And I will return to elaborate on this in recounting my experience in the Future Professor's Programme.

One is not promoted into the professoriate by knowing people in positions of power. Or is one? Perhaps this could be linked to the history of the discipline. Although a variety of intersections between race and class were associated with discrimination, what I learnt is that titles and position give little insight into who one is or what one is capable of. I interpret the way black interns were treated as a regression, especially working in a space led by an Indian professor.

After this experience, I would build my own table and God prepared it for me in the presence of my adversaries. I just knew it. God answers prayers. I was not intellectually stimulated at the science council because I was side-lined and mistreated. All the black staff knew that we needed to get out to grow elsewhere.

I applied for a research fellowship in Belgium through the European Union, and I was accepted. I was so relieved and handed in my resignation immediately. A new day dawned. It was time to heal. I was about to embark on a journey of self-discovery. I was going to Antwerpen in Belgium.

* * *

It was a real ordeal getting my family to Belgium. We had six months of paperwork that needed filing with the Belgian Consulate for immigration to Antwerpen. I was awarded a research fellowship at the University of Antwerpen in the Department of Epidemiology and Social Medicine. Professor van Hal was my mentor and sponsor.

We lived in the heart of Antwerpen which was within walking distance of the university and there were numerous pubs in our street. The fashion strip, the Meir, was a brisk five-minute walk from our home. Needless to say, it was a hustle and a bustle, a melting pot of cultures and nationalities.

I may be accused of having immigrated to the colonisers. In my opinion, I wanted to know what it was like to live in a first-world country, again. In all honesty, it was so unusual, it was unreal.

The Belgians are proud people. They expect you to learn their language and history to ensure a smooth assimilation into their culture.

Assimilation, again. It really disturbed my soul to assimilate into a culture which colonised my homeland. I instinctively knew that it did not sit well with my soul. It did not sit well with my values and sensibilities to assimilate in Belgium.

As part of my permanent residency agreement it was compulsory for me to participate in what they called *"inburgeringsklas"* (citizenship class). I was also forced to learn the language. Since I was fluent in Afrikaans (a creole-type derivative of Dutch), I was given a speed test to gauge at what level I needed to start the language course. I skipped two levels. In order for me to teach at a Belgian university I had to reach level 5 (native language speaker). Fortunately, I was able to teach international courses which were taught in English. But, as a permanent resident, I had to learn to speak Dutch even though I lived in Antwerpen where Flemish was the lingua franca. My Dutch language teacher was fascinated by my extensive Dutch vocabulary and I quickly became the teacher's pet for lack of a better phrase. My classmates were mostly refugees from Arabian countries and the Middle East. They really struggled with the language.

I was truly amazed by the drinking culture in Antwerpen. Sixteen is the legal drinking age and around three o'clock in the afternoon one would see teenagers chugging down beers by the pint. It offended me to be honest. They were a noisy bunch.

Getting lunch at the cafeteria was a culture shock. Seriously. The meals were gourmet, very tasty, but the drinks they offered near the checkout were shocking. I'm used to water and soft drinks being near the checkout; at the University of Antwerpen, one could purchase a bottle of wine or a beer off the same shelf as a coke. Universities were basically breeding alcohol abusers. At least that was my take on it.

Without a doubt, my most memorable experience whilst working at the University of Antwerpen was coordinating a study entitled "European University Students' Experiences and Attitudes Toward Campus Alcohol Policy: A Qualitative Study" (Van Hal et al., 2018). Working on European university student alcohol policy answered so many questions I had about this cultural nuance. Certainly, when I worked at Howard University and at South African universities, one would never find alcohol served in campus cafeterias.

I learnt so much from my colleagues in Belgium, Denmark, France, Hungary and the Slovak Republic about their students' alcohol over-consumption, and its adverse health consequences.

Living in Europe was not all work, work, work, though. My family and I had the opportunity to visit various countries such as France, the Netherlands, Germany and Italy. My oldest daughter celebrated her 12th birthday at Disneyland Paris. It was an enchanting experience to be able to afford my children international experiences I had not even dreamt of growing up in apartheid South Africa.

However, as generations become more open to diverse experiences, they also take much for granted. In fact, it turned out that my children did not enjoy living in Europe, and so we made plans to return home. In fact, my youngest wanted to return home after our first snowstorm in Antwerpen.

It was a bittersweet experience going back to South Africa. A mother is responsible for her children's happiness and I could not turn a blind eye to their daily struggles with the language and culture. We left Belgium in January and I started working at Rhodes

University in February. The children were happy to enrol in English schools. It reminded me of my experience moving to Cape Town after the torture of learning Afrikaans in Breidbach. My siblings and I were their age when my father uprooted us from Cape Town to Breidbach. I could completely identify with my children and therefore it was an easy decision to move back home.

I wanted to make the transition from an upbeat urban city (Antwerpen) to a rural province as smooth as possible, so we moved to Port Alfred, right on the beach. At least in Port Alfred there were some reminders of our life in Cape Town because of our proximity to the sea.

12

Psychology's unfinished business

Two historical figures cast long shadows over my becoming a psychologist. I was born on what has since been recognised in South Africa as Heritage Day, in September 1976. The same month that the Black Consciousness leader, Steve Biko, would be murdered by the apartheid regime in 1977. The same Biko who eloquently spoke on the psychological liberation of the subjective experiences of the black oppressed.

Just ten years earlier, Hendrik Verwoerd had been assassinated in the precincts of the white South African parliament during his term as prime minister. The same Verwoerd who believed in curtailing black education.

Both men are dead, but their contrasting ideas shaped and haunted my journey towards becoming a psychologist. This is psychology's unfinished business.

I was educated in a teaching practice designed to teach black learners to be hewers of wood and drawers of water for a white-run economy and society, regardless of an individual's abilities and aspirations. Given my education, and in light of the #FeesMustFall movement, there is no doubt that my teaching practice is under-pinned by higher education theories that address the post-colonial context and in which an integrated identity formation empowers the student to focus on critical self-reflection and, at the same time, prepares them for the workforce and enables them to contribute to transforming the society they live in.

Transformation in higher education is embedded in our nation's consciousness. As a strategy and as policy in post-apartheid South African universities, it is imperative in terms of what the country needs. Critical voices on transformation in South African universities have taken into consideration the radical diversification of students over the past two decades. It is against this backdrop that I contextualise my teaching and learning experiences in the discipline of psychology.

My journey with the transformation of higher education started in 1995, a year of expectation, the first year of our country's democracy. Since 1998, I had worked as a tutor, a teaching assistant, taught psychology, social work, and trained public health students in qualitative research methodology. All the positions I had occupied as a teacher were secured without prior experience and insight into how my students learn and how my teaching philosophy impacted them.

One thing that stands out when I reflect on my teaching practice is the way in which I tried to weave a web of my work experience within the curriculum. I did this consciously because I wanted to prepare my students for the job market, something I never benefited from.

The Bantu Education system might have ended long before our democracy, but its remnants are still experienced by most students today. For example, when I was studying at UWC, we did not have access to the same resources that students at UCT had. I realised this only when I taught students who had transferred from UCT to complete their Honours at UWC. The UCT students would moan the entire year about the lack of educational tools like software (which was very expensive).

And yet, the South African education system has transformed significantly over the years, notably in the 1990s which saw the abolition of the apartheid system and its separate education system for each of the population groups.

I remember that, as a 12-year-old, transitioning from an urban primary school in Cape Town to a rural school in King Williams Town, there appeared to be very little change in the daily routines of the different schools and classrooms I occupied. But the knowledge and exposure I had in Cape Town was significantly different in King. For example, I felt like I was repeating a grade but was taught in Afrikaans instead of English. Another change I experienced when transitioning from UWC to Stellenbosch University was access to resources. Simply put, the Stellenbosch University library had much better access to journals and books and search tools that UWC simply did not have. Professor Jansen (2002, p. 199) mentions something similar to my experience in primary and higher education:

> why is it that despite the production of literally thousands of pages of formal policy documents after apartheid, there is so little change in school and classroom practice throughout South Africa? I will not repeat the considerable evidence pointing to the policy–practice "gap" within South African education since the end of apartheid and the inauguration of a Government of National Unity in April 1994, led by the first President of a democratic South Africa, Nelson Mandela. What is lacking in the available literature are new explanations for this distance between policy and practice – other than the well-trodden assumption that "if only there were more resources", education reform in poor countries could expect greater fidelity between policy (what government officials intend) and practice (what actually happens in classrooms).

Against this backdrop of narratives such as the gaps between policy and practice, the inadequacy of teacher training, the weak design of implementation strategy, and the problems of policy coherence, I present my teaching practice. I do so by providing an example of a course I teach, and an explanation as to why I teach in the way I do.

I teach Critical Health Psychology (CHP) to third-year students who major in psychology at undergraduate level. Since most of my practical work experience has been in public mental health research and policy development, I am really in my element when I teach this course. In 2021, about 230 of my third-year psychology students engaged in compulsory online community-based service learning in the CHP course during the Covid-19 pandemic. I am attracted to community-based service learning because in my formative years my father instilled a deep-seated value of giving back. My father described his generosity as restorative: "Giving back means that you restore a space you once occupied by replacing your absence with a need that people have." There was a catch though, he cautioned: "Remember, giving must be sustainable."

Writing about the importance of community-based service learning I have reflected on my experience with my father's university residence students, and it led to a light-bulb moment. The time I felt most alive and productive was not in the classroom but when I worked with my father on his many outreach projects. This happened during my time as an undergraduate student and even more so in my Honours year. My father did not realise this then, but his passion towards volunteerism had been more than service delivery – it had taught me how to be a good citizen. Now, as a university lecturer, both my students and I experience first-hand how community-based service learning is implemented successfully when community partners benefit, and students learn.

Simply put, service learning is an educational tool whereby students use what they learn in the classroom and implement it within their social context (Akhurst et al., 2016). Service learning is embedded in the university's institutional mandate, and it is imperative that lecturers make use of this didactic tool. Community-based service learning is a form of practical learning in which students engage in activities that, in partnership with stakeholders, address community needs, together with well thought out opportunities designed to promote student learning and development (Akhurst et al., 2016). For example, students who major in psychology, partici-pate in community-based service learning and are in their final year of undergraduate studies, appreciate the personal growth and practical insight into theoretical constructs in the discipline.

More important is that community-based service learning amounts to citizenship education that contributes to the promotion of social justice, social reconstruction and democracy in the South African context (Dwomoh, 2021). Suffice to say, in the context of South Africa, critical citizen education is based on participation in the vision of the anti-apartheid struggle as presented in the Constitution of the Republic of South Africa (Enslin, 2003). The connection between citizen education and community-based service learning is simple: community-based service learning exposes students so that they can engage critically with how to practice their democratic citizenship and possess the values stipulated in the Constitution (Paulse, 2019).

For many undergraduate psychology majors, the odds of getting into a postgraduate programme are very slim. Out of a class of about 200, only about 40 are accepted into a postgraduate programme and it is strictly about the strength of a student's academic performance. Community-based service learning has the potential to enhance graduate employability skills and personal growth (Mtawa, et al., 2021). Community-based service learning also enhances graduate outcomes beyond the narrow premise of training graduates solely for employment – it reinforces social and civic responsibility.

Why is it important to prepare students to be socially responsible citizens and not only prepare them for a future career in psychology, especially during a global pandemic such as Covid-19? Educational countermeasures were taken to continue educating students despite the Covid-19 ramifications as tertiary educational activities switched to emergency remote (online) learning (Toquero & Talidong, 2020). We were like blind mice, feeling our way through a pandemic and making up emergency responses to an educational crisis – looking North, South, East and West. Nobody knew how to respond to the effects Covid-19 had on the academic project, and everybody was working through the darkness looking for a glint of light. As lockdowns increased and loosened in South Africa, we had to work around the problem and make the best out of a dire situation. This was when I decided to foster a sense of community and belongingness in my CHP class. Students were interacting with the community partners and myself via email, conducting virtual training workshops as the digital divide increased, socially and psychologically drawing closer towards understanding how to navigate through the trenches of the "new (ab)normal" global crisis.

Covid-19 took me back to a time when I had little to no access to resources and demanded that I think outside the proverbial box. This state of not knowing what was going to happen next and having no control over what the future held took me back to being black during apartheid. You might think: "How on earth can you compare the loss of human lives, jobs and sense of community to a biological threat?" Pause. Think about what apartheid did and compare it to Covid-19. As a nation we could not control the viral outbreak, but during apartheid, black people were controlled. Lockdowns, curfews, lack of employment all reminded me of the conditions under which black people lived during apartheid. If you were black and living in South Africa, you would know what I mean. If you weren't, may I suggest you read *Long Walk to Freedom* by Nelson Mandela (1994). Navigating through the Covid-19 pandemic whilst attempting to complete the academic project felt like a long, long walk towards uncertainty much like the walk towards freedom during apartheid.

It is important to contextualise that in South Africa, access to higher education is a contentious social justice issue. Long before the pandemic, South African universities were experiencing strain.

The #FeesMustFall movement is a recent example of the protests stemming from underfunding, interference and instability in South African universities (Jansen, 2017). Universities are constantly coerced to foster creativity as well as technical knowledge and, in the process, confronting their own limitations for new possibilities emerge (Trowler, 2018). Jansen's (2017) *As By Fire* predominantly presents quite a pessimistic view on the survival of the university. However, I do share Jansen's *ray of hope* that citizens (including academics and students) should recognise the value of the university and fight for its survival.

Fighting for the survival of the academic project was definitely what was needed during the Covid-19 pandemic. It created panic and chaos globally, yet, as an academic, I was driven to think more practically and creatively about the implementation of an online curriculum. Although 2020 was mostly about emergency response teaching, I learned painful lessons and was prepared to make significant changes to how I taught based on how my students learn in the online space. I decided to embed the CHP course within the community-based service-learning approach and the Sustainable Development Goals for health (Doctor et al., 2021).

My biggest concern for budding psychology students is that more than likely ninety per cent of every third-year class will not be selected for the Honours programme. This begs the question: What happens to that ninety per cent of psychology majors after they graduate, and when their hopes of becoming psychologists are shattered? The ninety per cent is the main reason why I structure my course to include a community-based service-learning component because the CHP course presents alternatives to traditional ways of being a mental health professional. The ten per cent is not left out of the course objectives because they get the opportunity to experience the profession they are entering into through service learning.

Given the large class numbers, it is quite challenging to run a community-based service-learning project single-handedly and therefore, in partnership with community leaders, ethical considerations and continuous monitoring and evaluation of appropriate short-term community-based service-learning projects were conducted. I wanted to create a curriculum that was both a reparative and transformative tool in a historical context that was plagued by the uncertainty of a deadly pandemic. In doing so, I developed a curriculum which was decolonialising dominant knowledges produced by Euro-American theoretical constructs of how we (both my students and I) understood the knowledge production processes of social change and social justice. Disrupting traditional, colonial pedagogues is key to transformation. Community-based service learning confronts the discomfort students have with non-traditional pedagogies.

In my experience, most students (especially academically high-achieving students) revolt against transformative pedagogues like community-based service learning. I think, in my experience, it is because community-based service learning is not common practice, sadly, and because it forces students to apply their minds. Most students who get high marks may not necessarily understand the work; they excel because of their good memories or study methods. So, when the bulk of the mark is about interpretation and critical reflection, students panic.

Class time is used to clarify and talk through learning experiences within their context. Arranging field visits and tours of health facilities, and designing service-learning projects which encourage students to use theoretical constructs to underpin their volunteer work are important learning outcomes. I believe that to address psychology's unfinished business, psychology students need to learn more outside of the classroom and unpack what is observed inside the classroom.

* * *

What follows is a personal account of what happens in South African universities. The experiences I refer to are not isolated to Rhodes University; they are based on corridor conversations amongst black academics, both male, female and gender nonconforming individuals globally, who are too afraid to be blacklisted or fired.

Dear Dr Jacobs,

Here are some of the screenshots from our psychology presentation WhatsApp group. Something had to be done, these students' anger and hatred is too much. I will inform you ma'am if anything extreme happens again.

– E-mail from an anonymous black student

In 2019, this email was written to me by a concerned black student in my third-year (exit level) CHP class. The three black students came to my office minutes before my CHP lecture. The students begged me to keep their identities anonymous because they were afraid that the white students in their tutorial group would harm them. The black students told me that there were WhatsApp messages in their group that were threatening my life. They wanted to warn me. Screenshots of the threats were emailed to me. An Afrikaner male student said: "Let's stone her." To which an Afrikaner female student responded: "I'll throw the first stone." After hearing this awful, unexpected news, I politely thanked the extremely anxious black students for bringing the threats to my attention and I tried with everything inside me to remain calm and collected in their presence. I reassured them that their identities would remain anonymous, but I would not allow these students to continue to antagonise them.

As soon as I shut the door behind them, I started shaking. I was in shock; I was angry, and I was confused. I had a thousand questions per second rushing through my mind. Some of these questions were: *What have these white students learned about gender-based violence in the past three years of their training in psychology? How has psychological training about race and gender affected their behaviour change? Why are white male and female students still resorting to archaic means of punishing black people when they do not get what they want? What calibre of whiteness are we sending into the workplace? How will these white students treat their black psych clients?*

My first response was to address the class about the anonymous tip. I was trembling with anger even as I was trying so hard to breathe and control my emotions in class. After telling the class what some of their classmates were planning to do to me because they did not want black students in their tutorial group, I ended the class. I told them I was in no state of mind to continue with the lecture.

I went back to my office and immediately wrote to my head of department (HOD) and the university's proctor. Emails were sent back and forth but very little came of it.

Let's unpack, not only my experience as a black female lecturer teaching critical psychology, but the anxiety experienced by the black third-year students through a critical social psychological lens using African feminist tools.

The hostility the white students projected towards their black classmates and their lecturer is a classic example of prejudice and inter-group conflict that has plagued South African society for hundreds of years. By the time my students reach their third year they are about to turn 20 or 21 years old. In 2019, these racist and sexist white students could have been born in 1998 or 1999. This means that their parents grew up during apartheid and most likely indoctrinated them to believe that they should form groups that are familiar (in-group) and alienate people who do not look like them (black people, the out group). So, let us go with the assumption that they were socialised to believe that what is black, is alien, inferior, lesser than white people.

This is not an implausible theory, given their "anger and hatred". Loyalty to the in-group meant the students trusted that the white male HOD would override whatever decisions are made in the classroom because of assumed mutual hatred for black people. This analysis comes straight out of Foster and Louw-Potgieter's (1991) book on social psychology in South Africa. Notably, Foster and Louw-Potgieter's publication was among the first texts on inter-group behaviour describing theoretical constructs of group dynamics in our context. The fear and anxiety experienced by my black students is an outstanding example of social identity theory and inter-group conflict. This example of prejudice and discrimination is highlighted by Kopano Ratele and Norman Duncan's (2003) book on *Social Psychology: Identities and Relationships*. Painstakingly, these are everyday stories of normalised systemic racism in higher education. This narrative account of "anger and hatred (is too much)" experienced by black students and black academics could be used as a tool for critical, participatory and socially transformative decolonialising methodologies.

I write about this experience as if it is the only one I've experienced working at historically whites-only universities. There are too many to list and, frankly, I am emotionally drained just writing about this recent account. Yet, when I feel psychologically attacked by my white colleagues and white students, the words of June Jordan (1980, p. 272), bring me solace: "We are the ones we have been waiting for."

So what if it seems as if the past and present South Africas are merging? So what if generational patterns of inter-group hatred and anger seem to have no end? The real questions we should be asking ourselves as academics, no matter what discipline you find yourself in, are: *Are we [black people] the only ones who need to teach and educate students about our country's history? And why are all psychology lecturers not incorporating diversity training in their classrooms?*

Decolonialising the academic environment means that we all must develop transformative curricula and not band-aids to breaking down barriers. For example, long ago, one of my Zimbabwean postgraduate students, during consultation, said that she was taking an Honours elective on social psychology, taught by a white male lecturer. She said that she was concerned that the lecturer did not contextualise the social psychological concepts within a South African or even

African socio-political backdrop. It is a reflection of the legacy of slavery and colonialism when white academics refuse to transform their curricula.

Frantz Fanon's (1991) seminal *Black Skin, White Masks* engages specifically with the recognition that our history of slavery and colonialism is critical. Its legacies are perpetuated in post-colonial social formations such as the inter-group conflict I experienced with my students in my CHP class. That is why it is so important to contextualise psychological concepts for our students. Yet, it appears that only black academics are employed to do this. A black colleague in confidence told me that the same white colleague who teaches social psychology asked him two years in a row to guest lecture on apartheid and contextualise the content of his course because he feels uncomfortable talking about it.

The email from the black students is testament to the aftermath of white lecturers refusing to do some heavy lifting, and getting out of their comfort zones. What is highlighted by this WhatsApp message is that academics need to close the racial divide in order to change the way in which students are taught since childhood that racists are bad people and that they simply are not bad. Students need to be taught that being less overt racists doesn't mean it's less bad. It's only more slippery, harder to identify, harder to report and harder to point to. Racism still kills people, takes away their rights, their dignity and their chance of having a fair shot at the lives we all deserve and that many take for granted.

This makes me realise that black academics are set up for failure. The "game" is rigged. The promotion process at some universities is set up in a way that puts black academics at an extreme disadvantage. An integral part of evaluating academics' teaching and learning abilities are the students' assessments of the lecturer. As most of the white students in my CHP class indicate, students have been shown to find black professors less credible than white professors.

13

1 in 9

I once did an evaluation of my social psychology class and most students wrote sentiments such as "black girl magic" but some wrote "resign before we get you fired". "They" (white students) told black classmates that they wished that I had died in an awful car accident so I could not give my last classes of the term. Generational patterns of inter-group "hatred and anger" are always just a stone's throw away in academia.

> *Let any one of you who is without sin be the first to throw a*
> *stone at her.*
> – John 8:7, New International Version

This phrase comes from an incident recorded in St John's Gospel, in the NIV Christian Bible. A group of men preparing to stone an adulterous woman to death were addressed by Jesus with these words (John 8:7, NIV, 2009). I am a black female academic threatened with stoning by, among others, a white female third-year student. Rereading a key biblical text regarding male violence against women to learn from Jesus on how to respond to it, led me to believe that Jesus must have been some kind of proto-feminist. A feminist is someone who supports equal rights for women. So, this self-righteous anti-feminist white female student felt justified in her threat to "throw the first stone". In her mind, she was "without sin". This perplexes me deeply. Where was she when Rhodes University gained national publicity for the 1 in 9 silent protest?

The 1 in 9 silent protest is a radical feminist stance to raise awareness of the alarming rates of violence (specifically, sexual violence) against women in this country. Rhodes University is at the forefront of gender activism in South Africa and various feminist campaigns are run throughout the year. The silent protest is a powerful feminist tool. I found myself very confused by the ease with which white third-year psychology students could make violent threats against their lecturer and get away with it.

Gender discrimination is the basis of masculine power and oppression of females. Despite the presence of revolutionary theories such as feminism, a black female lecturer is constantly threatened. The white male student who said "let's stone her" is the reason the goals of feminism cannot fully be realised under a flourishing patriarchy. Regardless of the race and gender dynamics in the classroom, women's subjugation has not been fully extinguished in higher education.

Feminists such as bell hooks (1984) believe that the only way to quell women's oppression is to end gender discrimination and the concept of masculinity as the superior gender. However, South Africa maintains a postmodern form of black oppression via white women to serve the interests of white South Africa.

The white female student who boldly exclaimed that she would "throw the first stone" reminds me of the Women's Ku Klux Klan (WKKK) in North America. Ruby Hamad's (2020) *White Tears/Brown Scars* engages an inquiry into white supremacy and the role of white women in it. Essentially, this is the white privilege demonstrated by racist and sexist white university students which is what I would like to address.

This is not a self-pitying rant with no way forward. No. What I learned from my many experiences with patriarchy is that within my authenticity lies my real power. Even in those environments which demand my complete and total assimilation. To the patriarchy I've been practically invisible. The patriarchy's arrogance is its greatest vulnerability and my greatest opportunity. *The only thing we have to lose is our chains.* They are stuck in the past. We are the future. Our time is now.

What you read in this book cannot be unread, overlooked or forgotten. I am inviting academe to confront this issue of white privileged "innocence" to sustain its prestige and credibility. This is not an attack on white feminists either. Instead, a close inspection of the white damsel and her tears that creates a dual status which is routinely weaponised against African feminists in South Africa and around the globe. A good example of this is when a white feminist in a department cries uncontrollably in a staff meeting because no one comes to a talk she has organised. African feminists like myself are targeted to rent-a-feminist crowd to attend white feminist talks. This is the systemic racist power white feminists in academe have over African feminists. It is the role they play in the vicious cycle of gender and race discrimination in South Africa. Chronic post-traumatic stress disorder and re-traumatisation are agenda-setting work and are a consequence of being victimised in academia because of your race and gender.

* * *

In 2020, when the world was turned upside down my life as a woman changed forever. Pelvic pain, abdominal pain, and bleeding for 18 months non-stop led me to a gynaecologist who told me: "You have three kids, given your age and the life-threatening condition of your uterus, I recommend that you have a full hysterectomy." I was drugged up with morphine post-biopsy and I agreed immediately to place my fate in the hands of a stranger.

It was a long and painful recovery process and needless to say the men that worked with me did not understand nor show any compassion. Since we were all under lockdown, I buckled up and decided to pre-record videos and start preparing to teach and coordinate courses. In no uncertain terms can I guarantee that, Covid-19 aside, 2020 was the worst year of my life. However, once again, the way I recovered from major surgery was to focus on my career. I distracted myself from the pain and remorseful regret, and channelled it into advancing my career.

> *Days were dark.*
> *We have to play our part to make our mark …*
> *[so], Excellent, finally a Black President to represent!*
> – Universal Souljaz (Prophets of Da City)

If you want to know where you are heading, you must remember where it all started. *Prophets of Da City* (POC) was an iconic and pioneering Cape Town hip hop group. Their lyrics were anti-apartheid and consequently banned in South Africa. When I was in high school, they would tour schools and edutain (using entertainment such as rap lyrics to educate) us about the liberation movement.

I was driving home from the office one day and I recalled their track "Neva Again". Nelson Mandela's famous words in his inauguration speech: "Never, never and never again shall it be that this beautiful land will again experience the oppression of one by another" (1994). It brought tears to my eyes. I felt an intense sense of responsibility. Captured, chained, discarded by the colonisers and apartheid government, there were not necessarily going to be a lot of opportunities for people who looked like me.

When I listened to POC's "Neva Again", I knew that something needed to change in the psychology department. For more than a hundred years the department had never had a black professor nor head of department. This saddened me because it implied that there had been little to no black representation (as alluded to by the POC lyrics quoted above). The head of department (HOD) position became available, and I was nominated by a few black colleagues to take it up. I think this shocked many of my other colleagues because I was a researcher. I never saw myself as an administrator. I was also new to Rhodes University and the department. As a loner, I was not part of a clique and, being a teetotaller, I skipped social drinks with colleagues. No one in the department really knew my stance on politics or policies, so I was a wild card.

The Dean of Humanities visited our department and asked us to email him our nominations, the only proviso being that the nominees had a PhD in psychology. This eliminated many people who might have wanted to take up the position because we didn't have many staff members that were qualified beyond master's level. Also, I was the only black woman with a doctorate in the department. If you go onto our department's website, you will find that historically HODs have been mostly white males. Only two white female professors were ever appointed as HOD. This means that my appointment as HOD of the psychology department, ratified at Council on 2 December 2021, was an historical moment.

Even though I know that with this position comes heavy responsibility administratively, I acknowledge that this is a *victrix ludorum* for black people. "We are the ones we have been waiting for" (June Jordon, 1980). On 2 December 2021 I was also promoted to associate professor in the Department of Psychology. I can only attribute this success to God's favour and the Future Professors Programme.

14

Future Professors Fellow

You are taught how to become a humanities scholar, but rarely taught, trained and mentored in a systematic way to become a professor ... It's always struck me as odd.
– Professor Jonathan D. Jansen

On 18 December 2020, I received a WhatsApp message that would change my career, catapulting it into a stratosphere I had thought existed only in my conversations with God. "Good afternoon, Dr Jacobs. I am JT, one of the lead implementers of the Future Professors Programme (FPP) and I just wanted to reach out to welcome you. Please feel free to save my number. I will call you later. Here is my email address ..." read the beginning of a life-altering experience in my academic career. Why? In my experience, distinguished professors are usually unapproachable and you certainly don't easily get access to their private cell phone numbers. Not only JT, but so many of the other professors in the FPP showed me kindness, care, respect and mentorship which I had always yearned for as a scholar. My prayers were answered in the FPP. How? The programme included scholars from across disciplines. I was one of two trained in psychology. As members of the FPP, we were a group of cheerleaders, champions and our life coach was godsent.

In the quote above, Distingushed Professor and A-rated scientist, Jonathan Jansen alludes to the point this chapter tries to make: no one teaches you how to become a professor. I'd like to add that nobody teaches you how to become a respected, ethical professor. In addition to Prof. Jansen's sentiment, my experience has taught me that being a professor means that you have to be arrogant, unaccessible and sometimes engage in unethical behaviour. The FPP lead implementers taught me that I needed to stay humble; be generous with my knowledge; show kindness, support and respect to colleagues and students.

I had always wanted to know what the recipe for becoming a professor, esteemed, respected and recognised internationally, was. Over the years, I had worked with many professors who'd held their cards close to their chests. It was as if becoming a professor was akin to joining an elite secret society. This changed when I received a letter from the minister of higher education and training welcoming me into the fold. Professor JT called me almost immediately after, and welcomed me to the programme. I was overwhelmed with happiness and gratitude.

The lives of South African academics were significantly impacted by the Covid-19 pandemic. The closure of schools and universities led to a shift in the education system, with a focus on relevant and responsive learning (Ramrathan, 2021). Universities faced challenges, including the need for mitigation strategies (Hedding et al., 2020). Young adults experienced disruptions in their leisure activities, but also displayed resilience and adapted to the changes (Wegner et al., 2022). These changes reflect the broader societal impacts of the pandemic on South African academics. My introduction to the Programme in 2021 was during the first year of the pandemic. In spite of the stress, depression and psychological pain members of the FPP were experiencing, our induction into the FPP during the initial Zoom sessions were a welcomed breath of fresh air. A reprieve from the isolating effects of the pandemic. Jeremiah's (Jeremiah 29:11, NIV, 2009) rhetoric of hope out of disaster comes to mind when I think of how impactful the FPP was.

To provide an even clearer understanding of the context in which the FPP was implemented in the early years of the pandemic, I need to highlight the role I played in my department. In 2021, I was a senior lecturer. With the assistance of the FPP lead implementers, I applied for a promotion. I was awarded an associate professorship during my first year in the FPP. I was also appointed head of department (department chair) in 2021. I began working in my new roles as associate professor and head of department in January 2022.

The role of head of department during the pandemic has been complex and challenging, requiring crisis leadership skills (Gigliotti & Fortunato, 2021). This period has called for a reorientation of academic practice, with a focus on care and a redefinition of excellence in teaching and research (Corbera et al., 2020). The pandemic significantly impacted the training experiences of psychology interns and postdoctoral fellows, with shifts to telehealth and virtual supervision (Gardner et al., 2021). Healthcare professionals, including those in psychology, have faced unique challenges during this time, such as redeployment, isolation and concerns about infection (McGlinchey et al., 2020). These studies underscore the need for department chairs to prioritise the well-being of their faculty and students, while also adapting to the changing landscape of academic and professional training.

At time of writing, I had been in the FPP programme for almost two years and it was hands down the most memorable of my career. The fellowship with others like me was heart-warming. The workshops we attended every Friday and the life-coaching sessions were life changing. The emphasis on the importance of excellence in teaching, research and service had me awestruck.

I know that my role as an HOD is the total opposite of what the FPP is designed to expose me to. At the back of my mind, I know that research, teaching and service learning are more paramount than my role as an HOD. But I also know that as HOD I have an obligation to my people, to pave the way for others.

Being the first black HOD and professor in a psychology department that is more than a century old is not something I find pride in. It is a sad reflection of the state of white institutions of higher learning. So, as HOD I will continue to teach my Critical Health Psychology course which is a service-learning course. And I will continue to publish on the topic. The Rhodes University Community Engagement Office has been very supportive in this regard.

You want to know the end? Look at the beginning. That drives me. The fact that I am here, a professor and an HOD of the psychology department, is testimony to the fact that I come from very resilient ancestors. Leaders grow their character when they face a choice between right and wrong and they choose right. The FPP leadership chose me, and I know that sets me ahead of the pack for life. Even when books do not provide the answers we seek, they can still help us to ask better questions. Nothing is worthless to an enquiring mind.

In the past, adversity left me breathless. Now I can breathe. The past voices of self-doubt and insecurity are silent. I accept myself. I am proud to be a Christian, African feminist, black South African and critical psychologist. I have the right to occupy spaces that require high intellectual functioning. I am good enough. I am strong. I am courageous. I am resilient and I will persevere. I am at peace.

I cannot in good conscience claim to have had a single bad experience as a fellow in the FPP. I cannot say the same about my personal life. I suffered great loss during my three years in the programme: my health took a turn for the worst and my father passed away. My belief is that writing about painful experiences can be a valuable tool for processing and healing from them.

Two years after my hysterectomy, in July 2022, I was in my friend's basement apartment in Washington, DC. I woke up one morning in excruciating pain and when I got to the bathroom all I saw was blood. I called another friend in a panic and told her what was happening. She rushed to me with enormous sanitary towels, a salad and some good old comfort conversation that only a girlfriend could give. She stayed with me until the friend I was living with came home from work. The two of them just allowed me to lie back and listen to their stories as a distraction from the agony. It felt like I was having a period, with the period pain and everything that goes with it. My ankles where swollen and my legs were in pain. I was worried. When I returned to South Africa, my doctor referred me to a radiologist and then referred me to a gynaecologist. I put this off until I had a conversation with one of the Future Professors Programme leads. She told me that it sounded like I may have endometriosis. She strongly recommended that I see a gynaecologist.

I was not thrilled but a couple of weeks after speaking with her I got a diagnosis. It was an awful experience. The doctor who performed my hysterectomy was not available, so I went to another female doctor. She was horrible. She did not believe that I'd had a hysterectomy. I was speechless, imagine me telling her I had fibromyalgia as well. And then she asked if I had been seeing a psychologist because I need to manage my stress!

She was still in disbelief that I'd had a hysterectomy. Without notice, she shoved the speculum into me – twice! Repetitively saying, "You have no uterus. Where is the blood coming from?" Only after an hour of internal inspection did she sit me down and explain that she needed to operate immediately. I refused. I asked if we could explore a non-surgical intervention first. She agreed and put me on Visanne. All while I had to run a department, mother three children and nurture myself. I dream of never being called resilient again in my life. I have found having to be strong exhausting. I want support. I want ease.

Do not pat me on the back for how well I take a hit or for how many hits I have taken. I want to embrace the beautifully broad spectrum of the human experience.

* * *

This section of the book I dedicate to the late Future Professor, Dr Rehana Malgas-Enus, chemical scientist at Stellenbosch University. On 21 September at 5:54 pm I received a call from Prof. JT. She apologised for calling me at that hour and I jokingly said that it is the best time because all my meetings for the day had ended. She interrupted politely and said: "Oh, Liezille, I have very bad news. Rehana died." I screamed: "No!" And JT's voice broke a little.

Within a split-second I immediately realised that poor JT had the unenviable task of calling the hundreds of Future Professors fellows to give them the same news and having to hear everyone's dreadful reactions on learning of the sudden death of our beloved Rehana. That was when I decided to stop reacting. I immediately sympathised with Prof. JT. I told her I would be thinking about and praying for her as she called every fellow to tell them the devastating news.

In true form, before we said our goodbyes, Professor JT said: "Liezille, all I can say to you is go kiss and hug your family, please." I did not tell her that I wasn't home. I was away, working. Yet, I could not stop thinking about Rehana and her loved ones. I prayed for everyone who was touched by Rehana. So full of life, young and so very talented. She commanded a room and would always make us laugh. Rehana was delightful and super intelligent. Her famous words were: "Stop waiting for things to happen, go out and make them happen!"

Rest in power, Rehana!

There were many ups and downs during my three years in the FPP, the passing of a dear fellow, Rehana, was the worst.

The FPP closing ceremony and graduation were held on 29 February 2024, a Thursday. The Future Professors Programme has been instrumental in my personal and professional growth, and I am deeply grateful for the opportunity of having participated in it. The programme's emphasis on transforming values into action and inspiring a shared vision has been particularly impactful, as it has helped me develop a strong sense of purpose and direction. The collaborative learning approach and focus on developing professional skills have also been invaluable, enabling me to enhance my professional leadership capabilities in a practical and sustainable way.

I am especially thankful for the programme's emphasis on the biblical foundation for leadership, even though it may have been an unconscious or unintended consequence, which has provided me with a strong ethical framework for my leadership journey. The programme's emphasis on humble leadership behaviours has also been transformative, helping me to cultivate a leadership style that is both effective and empathetic. Thank you FPP for the opportunity of participating in this programme and for the ongoing support and guidance.

The FPP story is not finished because I am now an alumna of a prestigious, successful and impactful group of intellectuals who will continue to share our collective consciousness until the end.

PART TWO

Jacobs on autopsychobiography

It is important to note the difference between a biographer and a psychobiographer. Both are interested in the life story of an individual. The psychobiographer, however, applies psychological theories to interpret the biographical information (Fouche & Van Niekerk, 2010).

Psychobiography is a research method that explores the lives and personalities of public figures. It was originally developed by Sigmund Freud and gained popularity in the first half of the 20th century. However, it declined in popularity until the narrative turn in psychology brought about a revival of psychobiography in the 1990s. Contemporary psychobiography integrates psychoanalytical, personological and narrative perspectives, and has expanded its focus beyond artists to include scientists, politicians and historical figures.

This book is an autopsychobiography because it systematically formulates a life history and interprets it by means of psychological theories (Kovary, 2011; Manganyi, 2013, 2016; Mathabe, 2018; Schultz, 2005).

I drew inspiration from the psychobiography approach because it enabled me to examine the influence of the historical, societal and political factors of my development as a critical psychologist.

And since my training is in the discipline of psychology, it would be remiss of me not to draw on psychosocial theoretical accounts of development.

I also drew inspiration from autobiographers such as Paul Ricoeur (1981), Edmund Husserl (1983) and fellow South African psycho-biographer, Professor Manganyi (2013). What I learnt from these thinkers is the importance of interpreting one's *own* life story in terms of time and place (see Bronfenbrenner, 2005, chronosystem). According to Schultz and Lawrence (2017, p. 435), psychobiography "always starts with biography", that is, the facts of my life as I interpret them to be.

I therefore chose *auto*psychobiography as a method to describe my life story. It is an interpretative approach. Given that there is no one positivistic truth possible in psychobiography, I was drawn to this method because it allowed me to make connections, and because it drew on my talent of reading people. This reminds me of my father. He always said that to make psychology relevant in my daily life I must use psychological theory to read people.

I am in Paris, France in the summer of 2022. It has been a long trip away from home. The airport and Parisian streets are buzzing with different accents and languages I do not understand. I have a 23-hour layover. My first trip to Paris was in 2014 and I was mugged in Europe for the first time. So, I thought about my father's advice, to use psychological theory to read people. I was not going to fall prey to another haggler trying to distract me. On this particular trip, I spent most of my time in the US capital city. I met with African American women, among whom one had been the first minority to be a full professor in her field, another, a provost and heading up university departments. I realised that these women had made great strides towards transforming higher education in America.

To find the relevance of psychology in South Africa, being the first black head of the psychology department at Rhodes University meant that I needed to write my story before I forgot my father's wise instruction, to use psychology to my advantage, to use psychology to read people. So, being written in the midst of my father's dementia, this book, this autopsychobiography, has filled a void, and is proof that lives are not lived in laboratory conditions. The lives of the deceased enable us to trace personality development. A constantly changing life helped me to trace my most intimate way of being-in-this-world and made me feel alive. Unpacking my life story made me feel consensual validation in ways strictly clinical case studies never could.

The main aim for this autopsychobiography was to reveal not only who I am, but why and how I know what I do. On an epistemological note, the aim of my autopsychobiography is driven by an African feminist perspective which might resonate with some readers. Others plunging through psychological theories that purport to explain why I've experienced life as I have, will find a kaleidoscope of trauma and resilience. Transforming my way of being-in-this-world as opposed to subscribing to a cookie-cutter psychological theory, African feminism allows me the freedom to express my story through my memories. In this autopsychobiography I am reclaiming my story from Euro-American psychological personality frameworks. In this autopsychobiography I explore my ever-changing identity development from postcolonial and indigenous feminist standpoints, which challenged me to redefine my roles as feminist-activist educator and researcher working with formerly colonised and historically marginalised communities. As an African and black feminist, in this autopsychobiography I (re)construct my context-specific knowledge of an African women's power via relational world views of motherhood, family, sisterhood and friendship (Chilisa & Ntseane, 2010).

Theory

According to Schultz and Lawrence (2017), a psychobiography is best understood as a branch of applied personality science in which findings are used to describe an individual's life story. Usually this means that the individual and subject is familiar, famous and exceptional.

In South Africa, an array of exemplary personalities constitutes a hall of fame. Their legendary lives are ideal case studies which may be used to develop and/or refute aspects of psychological theory and its applicability to human development over the span of an individual's life.

This book breaks with the norm of psychobiographies because, in South Africa, psychobiographies are rarely done in the first person. Psychobiography entails the study of historically significant and extraordinary individuals over their *entire* lifespan to uncover and reconstruct their lives psychologically (Fouche & Van Niekerk, 2010). An autopsychobiography is a self-narrative methodology with humanistic psychology at its core: it recognises a human as a whole person, and it is framed in a narrative manner. By writing an autopsychobiography, I disrupt the notion that the psychobiographical approach is exclusively applicable to the analysis of famous personalities, and that it cannot be used productively to examine a life-in-progress.

My story, my voice – this is what the method provided as an analytical tool. I could tell my story and gain insights into my life using a systematic approach. I am not merely trying to change the way my story has been told by others, I am also transforming my "sense of what it means to live" (Bhabha, 1994, p. 256). I am driven by a postcolonial appeal which insists that if I wish to imprint my own way of life into the discourses that pervade the world around me, then I can no longer allow myself to be spoken on behalf of or to be subjugated by the hegemonies of others. This is not simply about establishing a new narrative.

As a research method, autopsychobiographies disrupt the inscribed binary between science and art, between theory and the imagination, and between rationality and emotion (Ellis et al., 2011). The method is not an instrument through which to seek validation, approval, assurance or vengeance. Although, of course, it might be possible for readers to feel a resonance, a sense-making, even validation by reading their own experiences in mine.

In one sense, therefore, I am leaning into and reclaiming my own story, not through the theorised conjecture of others, but through my own memories and witnessing. In another sense, I am countering and disrupting conventional approaches to research, which persist in claiming that research is somehow neutral and impersonal, and that it is possible for a researcher to stand outside of her research. According to Ellis et al. (2011, p. 274), a "psychobiography is one of the approaches that acknowledges and accommodates subjectivity, emotionality, and the researcher's influence on research, rather than hiding from these matters or assuming they don't exist".

Psychobiography was invented by psychoanalyst, Sigmund Freud (1964), while investigating the psychological determinants of Leonardo da Vinci's artistic creativity. Thereafter, more than 300 psychobiography's were conducted. The main pushback on and eventual rejection of this method was that it highly depended on psychological theory (Schultz & Lawrence, 2017). In this regard, psychological biographies offer an expansive lens on the world, steering away from rigid definitions of what constitutes meaningful and useful research (Ellis et al., 2011). Ponterotto (2015), critiques the psychobiographical method on the basis of its reliance on a single clue or coming to conclusions on inadequate data. Another criticism is that Freud over-identified with and projected his own unconscious struggles onto Leonardo's life (Schultz & Lawrence, 2017). Bearing in mind the criticisms of psychobiography, this book considers a point made by Elms (1994, p. 13):

> Lives are not lived in the laboratory. In the real world, personalities are not divided into statistically analyzable compartments. Experimental and correlational studies, and statistical analyses of the data they generate, may identify significant variables in the lives of people-in-general. But I haven't encountered a psychologist yet who could put together

*a whole person from those statistical body-parts and honestly
cry out, "It's Alive!"*

Since autopsychobiographies broadly fall within the narrative
research paradigm, Fouche and Van Niekerk (2010) argue that this
should encourage South Africans to conduct autopsychobiographical
research using themselves as research participants. This, however,
will somewhat present autopsychobiographical research as post-
paradigmatic because autopsychobiographies do not neatly fit into a
gestalt form of narratology (Dhunpath, 2000).

Research questions

The following research questions guided my autopsychobiography:

1. What do I want to know about my past and present?
2. Of what interest is my story to people other than myself?
3. How would sharing my life story in this way help further the
   wider understanding of other similar types of people?
4. How will conducting the autopsychobiography harm me or
   my family in any way?
5. How sufficient is the information available concerning my life
   story?

While not specifically a research question, I also seek to disrupt
the notion that only exceptional individuals can be the subjects of
psychobiographies to discover whether my autopsychobiographical
record may encourage postgraduates and other academics to tell
their own stories.

Methods

This autopsychobiography utilised at least four characteristics
common to psychobiographical research, including:

1. Collecting qualitative data.
2. Taking a comprehensive approach to the study of a life story.
3. Identifying myself and all the key role players by name (or pseudonym in some instances to protect people's privacy).
4. Disrupting the notion that the process should only utilise biographical data collected by other researchers.

The following steps were used as a guide to conduct this auto-psychobiography (Miles et al., 2014, p. 14):

Step 1	Select a subject.
Step 2	Identify primary and secondary sources relating to the subject. Critically evaluate the potential usefulness of these sources.
Step 3	Identify the context in which the subject lived and determine the amount of contextual data that is needed for the psychobiography. Access this data.
Step 4	Select appropriate psychological theory/theories.
Step 5	Allow the data to reveal itself (using Schultz's markers of psychological salience).
Step 6	Ask the data-specific questions relating to the subject being studied.
Step 7	Develop coding strategies and code the data accordingly. Multiple coding strategies will usually be necessary.
Step 8	Select display formats (use multiple formats if at all possible).
Step 9	Integrate coding with display.
Step 10	Write up the psychobiography.
Step 11	Revise the psychobiography in relation to specific questions developed (Step 6).
Step 12	Evaluate the research process.

Table 2: Step-wise approach of psychobiography (du Plessis, 2017, p. 222)

Phase	Steps	
Data collection	Step 1	Select a subject
	Step 2	Identify primary and secondary sources relating to the subject. Critically evaluate the potential usefulness of these sources.
	Step 3	Identify the context in which the subject lived, and determined the amount of contextual data that is needed for the psychobiography. Access this data.
	Step 4	Select an appropriate psychological theory/theories.
Data condensation	Step 5	Allow the data to reveal itself (using Schultz's markers of psychological salience).
	Step 6	Ask the data specific questions relating to the subject being studied.
	Step 7	Develop coding strategies and code the data accordingly. Multiple coding strategies will usually be necessary.
Data display	Step 8	Select display formats (use multiple formats if at all possible).
	Step 9	Integrate coding with display.
Conclusion drawing and verification	Step 10	Write up of psychobiography.
	Step 11	Revision of psychobiography in relation to specific questions developed previously.
	Step 12	Evaluation of research process.

Data collection

According to Miles et al. (2014, p. 14), steps 1 to 4 incorporate the systematic process of data collection.

Step 1: Select a subject
This part of the autopsychobiography would in traditional research be referred to as the sample and sampling strategy. However, in this autopsychobiography, I was the main participant and reflecting on the past and present allowed me to make connections and clearly articulate the facts of my life. The autopsychobiography *is* the sample.

Step 2: Identify primary and secondary sources relating to the subject.
Critically evaluate the potential usefulness of these sources
One of the core concerns when conducting psychobiographical studies is the availability of a suitable quantity and quality of data to allow the study to progress (Schultz, 2005). An autopsychobiography does not warrant this because the *subject* is inferred to be the researcher/author. So, much like other autobiographical research such as autoethnographical studies, I would not be writing this book if I did not have a good recollection of how I came to be. Studying psychology and my incessant need to know more, learn more about why I do what I do and why others treat me in a particular way, my voice – my story provides insight into various psychological aspects of my psychological functioning. In particular, it is vitally important that at least some of the subject's own words are available (as a primary data source) since, according to Alexander (1990, p. 12), "adequate samples of the written or recorded oral productions of the subject constitute a major vein of source material." General guidelines for case-study research can assist in determining which data sources should be used. Yin's (2003) criteria related to the necessity of using multiple data sources, the construction of a database to manage the material collected, and the maintenance of a chain of evidence in relation to the analysis of the sources used are valuable as guidelines for this step of the research process. In particular, this step involves:

- Identifying as many data sources as possible, including existing data that have already been published as well as data that could be generated for the purposes of the project, for example, new interviews. Each potential source should be entered into a database. This database should ideally form a comprehensive bibliography of every available piece of information regarding a subject. However, with certain subjects this will not be possible (e.g., creating a comprehensive database of all writing on a subject such as Nelson Mandela would prove impossible due to the sheer volume of available material). In such cases, the psychobiographer must ensure they are aware of all seminal texts relating to the subject.

- Determining which of these sources to include in the project. The project should include a variety of sources that are able to provide a broad spectrum of information regarding the subject. This serves as a form of triangulation (Patton, 2002; Willig, 2008; Yin, 2009). The reasons for the inclusion/exclusion of specific sources must be made clear. So, for example, the inclusion/exclusion of artistic or literary works must be explained, as must the decision to generate new data/rely exclusively on existing data.

- The material that has been included must be clearly identified, and clear indications made regarding the strengths/limitations of this material. Thus, for example, the inclusion of literary works may potentially allow for the discussion of unconscious conflicts, but has the limitation of being open to numerous contradictory interpretations. In addition, possible biases within the collected material must be clearly highlighted. For example, work on prominent religious figures may be influenced by the author's own religious leanings (Saccaggi, 2015) as well as by a desire to venerate the religious figure (Mitchell & Howcroft, 2015). The decision regarding what data to include/exclude is crucial since it determines the nature of the psychobiography that can be produced. Since this is an autopsychobiography, Part One is an illustration of primary sources relating to my being-in-this-world. Secondary sources, being that I am not a famous person, are not easily accessible unless I had conversations with my mother to clarify my lived experience, my research publications, media articles written about my opinions on substance use disorder and gender studies.

Step 3: Identify the context in which the subject lived and determined the amount of contextual data that is needed for the psychobiography. Access this data

Part One of this book describes the context in which I lived in great detail. My early memories of living in Rocklands, Mitchell's Plain, moving to Breidbach, King William's Town, and back to Cape Town, the intersection between various biographical (personal) and historical events (such as apartheid and post-apartheid) and allows my life to be viewed in full socio-cultural context. Step 3, identifying the context in which my life is lived, and the depth of contextual data that was needed was a useful tool for this autopsychobiography. Part One of this autopsychobiography used a multi-layered chronological methodology to identify various stages in my development and showed how these intersected with various historical events and contexts in my life.

Step 4: Select an appropriate psychological theory/theories

The last phase in data collection relates to the selection of an appropriate theoretical lens through which to interpret the data collected. This step forms part of the decision regarding which theory to use and informs the data analysis process.

> *I came to theory because I was hurting – the pain within me was so intense that I could not go on living. I came to theory desperate, wanting to comprehend – to grasp what was happening around and within me. Most importantly, I wanted to make the hurt go away. I saw in theory a location for healing.*
> – bell hooks, 1991

bell hooks spoke the words quoted above durring a presentation at the conference "Breaking bread: Insurgent black intellectual life" in 1991. It is not hyperbole to say that bell hooks blessed me and so many women in a way only she could. It is because of her life's work that I embed my life story within the scope of an autopsychobiographical approach. bell hooks broke down boundaries and paved the way for academics to challenge everything – including methodology and theoretical underpinnings. hooks believed that children made the best theorists. Imagine, me, as a young girl wondering why I grew up without spending quality time with my father because he worked out of town most of the time. Imagine, trying to make sense of why my mother was home, pregnant, cooking, cleaning, minding the children when my father was away from home. Imagine, me, getting punished every time I asked my mom why she didn't work. Why my father was the only adult providing financially. Feminist theory presented itself in true form to me for the first time when an Anglican female priest asked me why I had trouble reciting the "Our Father".

The current state of feminism does make me wonder whether I can still call myself a feminist. African feminism, the feminist approach I feel most at home with, is rooted in the activist notion that we should eradicate oppression that affects all women, especially from the African diaspora. African feminism provides a satisfactory explanation for all my functioning and being-in-this-world.

I also drew on Bronfenbrenner's bioecological systems theory and Erikson's psychosocial theory of development. Bronfenbrenner's (1979) original diagram of concentric circles was called the ecological systems theory, and revolved around the child, with influences such as parents, peers, teachers, community members, and the greater societal values and views. The psychosocial theory of development was critically reviewed and referred to as a Euro-American paradigm to explain and reflect on my chronological psychosocial development. There were critical periods in my lifespan where I could not neatly fit into a gestalt form of Erikson's psychosocial developmental theory. It was in these moments that I not only critiqued the theory but also provided insight to possible adjustments to the theory.

Following the four data collection steps described above (selecting a subject, identifying data sources, identifying the context, and selecting a theory), the next steps of the autopsychobiographical research process relate to data condensation and data display.

In an attempt to detail how meaning is found within qualitative data, it is important to explain how coding for analysis of data is done in this instance. In qualitative data analysis, a code is a researcher-generated construct that is symbolic, and attributes interpreted meaning to each individual datum for later purposes of pattern detection, creating categories, and other analytic processes. Just as a title represents the contents of a book, so a code represents and captures a datum's primary content and essence (Saldaña, 2021). Qualitative data have three different coding strategies namely, deductive coding, inductive coding and a combination approach (Linneberg & Korsgaard, 2019). Deductive coding is when one starts off with a set of codes and sticks with them; inductive coding is when one comes up with the codes as one reads what one sees in the data and a combination of deductive and inductive coding is the combination approach (Linneberg & Korsgaard, 2019). Before coding in qualitative research, you should decide if you want to start off with a set of codes and stick with them (deductive coding), come up with the codes as you evaluate what you see in your data (inductive coding), or take a combination approach. Steps 5, 6, 7, 8 and 9 will describe the coding process.

Step 5: Allow the data to reveal itself
According to du Plessis (2017, p. 227), data can be coded to include markers that identify incidents that "fit" and data that "do not fit well in the identification of incidents". In this way, during the coding process, restructuring the data will result in the psychological aspects of the data emerging. For example, Alexander argues that these "identifiers of salience," are by no means exhaustive nor necessarily overlapping (1988, p.269). The identifiers used to code this autopsychobiography were primacy (the foremost identifier to describe my culture, language, rituals); frequency (I was attuned to

frequency or repetition as increasing signs of certainty); uniqueness (as a salience indicator is clearly related to a variety of normative behaviour – what must inevitably be kept in mind in invoking this criterion are the nomothetic baselines that emanate from general cultural expectations); negation (in Piagetian theory, a mental process – a form of reversibility – in which one realises that any operation can always be negated or inverted), emphasis (markers of major attention drawn to an event or happening and the lack of emphasis on important psychological processes); omission (instances in which I identify salient role players but describe everyone except for identifying significant friends or family members, this was coded); error (could be signalled by incredibility or overvaluing a relationship with a significant parental figure and undervaluing myself, for example); isolation (as a mark of salience, isolation is best recognised by the criterion of whether in reading or listening, one finds oneself asking what the connection is of one occurrence to another, what's missing), and incompletion (when a narrative flow is interrupted or when no closure is achieved).

Step 6: Ask the data specific questions relating to the subject being studied
In extracting the main psychological aspects of the data, the next step is to transform the salient extractions now that I have introduced a set of markers through which the initial data can be sorted and consequently reduced (Alexander, 1988). The generation of data can be addressed through the identification of specific research questions in relation to the psychobiography (du Plessis, 2017). Alexander (1988) suggests asking the data questions as a second step in his psychobiographical approach. In the approach advanced here, the questioning begins only after the collection of data has been completed; only when all available data have been collected does it become possible to know exactly what questions should be asked.

Alexander (1988) states that this method is not restricted to "any particular kind of question or any significant consequent mode of analysis" (p. 287). He does, however, suggest that the investigator provide the steps of reasoning that would allow an answer to the proposed question (Alexander, 1988, 1990).

In this book all the material gathered about and by me in Part One was subjected to the process of "questioning the data". Specific questions were designed based on both the theoretical approaches employed in this book as well as the objectives and aims of the research.

In my autopsychobiography, I asked critical questions pertaining to my identity with the following two questions in mind:

1. How will a dialogue be created between the extracted data and the content of the integrated theory guided by Urie Bronfenbrenner's (1986) ecological systems theory to understand my upbringing, specifically interactions with my environment and society over extended periods of time? This was addressed in Chapter 1 of the book.

2. How is psychosocial development conceptualised in this study? This was addressed throughout the first part of the book to illustrate how lifespan developmental theories such as Erikson's psychosocial theory do not always aid as all-encompassing explanations of my development as an African. This is noteworthy because most South African researchers and academics are working hard to decolonialise our understanding of being in this world (Hook, 2002).

I critique Erikson's theory in parts of my own development to prove how my developmental milestones do not necessarily fit neatly into Erikson's framework. My lifespans throughout both apartheid and post-apartheid eras in South Africa.

Step 7: Develop coding strategies and code the data accordingly
Coding is a qualitative data analysis strategy in which some aspect of the data is assigned a descriptive label (deductive coding) and allows the researcher to come up with the codes as they read what they see

in their data (inductive coding), or take a combination approach. The abovementioned steps 5 and 6 provided different coding strategies (psychological salience and targeted questioning) and a third strategy, thematic coding (see Braun & Clarke, 2006), can also be employed. According to du Plessis (2017), the point of this step is to re-arrange the data in multiple ways in order to allow aspects that are salient to psychobiographical research to emerge.

These three steps all involve rearranging the data in a manner that allows for various aspects of the data to emerge. The coding strategies for this research were initially decided upon following the specific theories selected previously; considering the concrete questions. I was always open to the possibility of including new content that might come up during the second reading stage, that is, psychological salient content. First, it was necessary to build a chronology of my first years until my young adulthood, always fact-checking recollections of my childhood with my mom. Second, helped once more by markers of psychological salience, these categories were decided upon to analyze the bioecological systems that have constituted my development: Rocky times in Rocklands; Displacement and the worst day of my life; Bad times in Breidbach; Living in two dimensions.

Step 8: Select display formats
A decision must be taken regarding the way in which the raw data will best be displayed for analysis and how the psychologically relevant information will be presented. There seem to be two main ways, either as a chronology or as only the salient themes (du Plessis, 2017). I decided to list both (see in relation to step 3 Chapters 2, 3, 4 and 5).

Step 9: Integrate coding with display
The coding strategy conducted in the previous steps is integrated with the display format in this step. When integrating the coding and the display, it is salient to represent a core aspect of the data

transformation since the coding and the display of data present biographical and other material in a manner that allows it to be interpreted from a psychological perspective (du Plessis, 2017). After the abovementioned steps are completed, the research findings are written up.

Conclusion and verification

Step 10: Write the autopsychobiography
Usually, in traditional research, the writing up of research findings happens at the end of the manipulation of data, in a step-wise approach. This autopsychobiography clearly disrupts the nature of a neatly conducted qualitative research project. In an ideal research laboratory in psychology there is a subject and a researcher. The questionable power dynamics that attend labelling a human being a "subject" predate the current research project. Going back to a famous research subject – Saartjie Baartman. Her genitals and other organs were studied by a zoologist. As a humanist psychological researcher, I discredit such power dynamics.

Part One of this book is both the beginning and the iterative outcome of the write-up. In section 2, I have described how I actually went about writing the autopsychobiography presented in Part One, including the ideal 12-step sequence of stages involved in the construction of my autopsychobiography. In reality, the process was quite circular (rather than sequential) in nature. However, I do agree that this autopsychobiography should focus on the psychological significance of my life story, thus the decision to not strictly follow the sequence set out by Miles et al. (2014) in the autopsychobiographical research process. In fact, the writing process is likely to have as many characteristics of art as it does science (Schultz, 2005).

This autopsychobiography has both artistic and scientific merit because it is an attempt to make psychology relevant in the South African context and an attempt to contribute to decolonialising the discipline of psychology.

Step 11: Revision of the autopsychobiography in relation to specific questions developed previously

The main aim of this autopsychobiography was unpacking not only who I am but why and how I know what I do. This autopsychobiography attempted to answer the following primary research question: What do I want to know about my past and present?

Before I studied psychology, I wanted to become an investigative journalist. I love dissecting a problem and coming up with possible solutions. I would journal about why my family had so many secrets and come up with weird scenarios.

Psychology gave me a scientific perspective for understanding what I needed to know about my family and my positionality within the family system. Imagine, a pre-pubescent girl being sexually molested by a trusted family member, who later in life develops endometriosis, experiencing sharp, numbing pain in the pelvis every day. This question was answered through perspicacity and the ability to make psychological connections; basically, interpreting my lived experience through a psychological lens.

Franz Alexander and his colleagues at the Chicago Institute of Psychoanalysis in the 1950s and 1960s suggested that specific personality traits and specific conflicts may create particular psychosomatic illnesses. I am not a fan of the psychoanalytic perspective. Its work focuses too much on pathologising.

Psychosomatic disorder describes the external manifestation, mainly through physical health, of primarily mental stressors. They are psychological conditions involving the occurrence of physical symptoms, usually lacking a medical explanation (for example, all autoimmune diseases). People with this condition may have excessive thoughts, feelings or concerns about the symptoms – which affects their ability to function well.

As a person who has been diagnosed with both fibromyalgia and endometriosis, I can attest that psychogenic medicine is an underdeveloped area in both medicine and psychology. The concept of psychosomatic disorder has been strongly criticised by people like me who are constantly labelled as "crazy" when we present symptoms of illnesses the causes of which are not yet known to medicine and science. The concept of psychosomatic disorder perpetuates the obsolete notion of psychogenesis, which is incompatible with multi-causality, a core postulate of current psychosomatic medicine. Psychosocial factors may vary from one individual to another who suffers from the same illness and underscores the basic conceptual flaw of considering diseases as homogeneous entities.

My suggestion to psychosomatic medics is to develop interventions that are comprehensive and interdisciplinary in their framework for:

- assessment of psychosocial factors affecting individual vulnerability, course and outcome of any type of disease;
- holistic consideration of patient care in clinical practice; and
- integration of psychological therapies in the prevention, treatment and rehabilitation of medical disease (psychological medicine).

Of what interest is my story to people other than myself? I wrote this book with the following people in mind: my parents, my siblings, extended family, friends, colleagues, acquaintances and my students. This book is written for everyone who is interested in: the academic project, the factors that influence apartheid's aftermath, the struggles that women (especially black) experience (in and outside of academia), future psychologists, and current academic and professional psychologists. In this book I write about how I became, against all odds, a champion of the post-apartheid struggle, a mother, and an academic in the field of critical and social psychology.

How would sharing my life story in this way help further the wider understanding of other similar types of people? Something I learnt early in my career as a budding psychologist was that in academia, what is done for us without us is not for us. Much like our ancestors, black women in academia (or any other male dominated profession) are still captured, chained and discarded. Applying for a job or a promotion feels like reliving slavery because we are an inconvenience. But we are the children of those who chose to survive. That gives us a powerful responsibility. As a black woman, my autopsychobiography is driven by an African feminist perspective which might resonate with some readers. Understanding my story is to ingress in my mind, a time capsule of a period before I existed. A time I am tethered to because of the lived experiences of my parents and that of theirs.

How will conducting the autopsychobiography harm me or my family in any way? In this book I used pseudonyms to protect people's identities. It is very important to me that people do not try to decipher the particular real-world identities of the personalities featured herein but rather focus on what it tries to achieve. This book is a form of self-reflection and my writing explores my personal experiences to make connections that are both historically significant and contextually interpreted.

It is my opinion that publishing this book will not harm my family in any way but celebrate its survival. A famous metaphor that we often repeat is that an arrow can only be shot by pulling it backward. So, when life drags me back, I imagine that I will be launched into something great.

How sufficient is the information available concerning my life story? In this book I share identity narratives that have enabled me to reflect on who I was, who I no longer am and who I became. Writing an autopsychobiography has been transformative and life changing because it forced me to evaluate my past, present and future in a way that is so profoundly intimate and self-soothing at the same time.

This book is about how my background (childhood, adolescence and adulthood) led me to become a doctor and professor in psychology. This is my personal account of how my generation (born in 1976, a turbulent time in South African history), became the first cohort (registered at university to become a psychologist in 1995) of free psychologists in post-apartheid South Africa. I embed my life story within the scope of an autopsychobiographical approach and interpret it by means of psychological theories like critical, psychosocial, personality psychology and African feminism.

Step 12: Evaluation of research process
Foremost, autopsychobiographies are not popular in South African psychological research. Truth be told, most positivist researchers do not believe in the validity of the psychobiographical research.

So, why would positivists give an autobiographical approach a second glance? Whenever someone, especially a black person, re-imagines what the discipline of psychology could look like if one coloured outside the lines, practitioners are quick to flip open their laptops and tear autopsychobiography to pieces without presenting an alternative approach. If you are *that* person, I appeal to you to take a deep breath and imagine that you, too, can let go of the fear of mechanically following a structured set of guidelines producing technically sound research that lacks the creativity and liveliness that is so characteristic of the discipline.

As critical psychologists we need to develop our own voices to protect the creative nature of the discipline – remembering why we critiqued mainstream psychology in the first instance.

My autopsychobiography is a guideline for research psychologists who are eager to plough into a creative scientific approach.

Conclusion

> *your own experience is a valid part of your own knowledge, as long as it is subject to public critical appraisal. And any way, it is your OWN understanding and practices you are trying to improve.*
> – Dhunpath (2000, p. 548)

The emergent self-narrative of this autopsychobiography achieves a richness of depth which empirical research involving larger samples is unlikely to yield. Although I did not use a personality trait analysis, which is common in psychobiographies, like those done by Sigmund Freud and Abraham Maslow, I opted for a multi-methodological empirical approach. Irrespective of the life story methodologies I used, what is important to note is that it all boiled down to how I interpreted my life story. Interpretation is the criterion of evaluation best suited for psychobiographies.

This autopsychobiography was a personal account of my life story to date, connecting my narratives to personality developmental theory and analysing it through an African feminist lens. The goal of the autopsychobiography was to study the psychological trajectory of my life during apartheid and post-apartheid South Africa. When I sat down to write this book, the goal was to educate people about what women like me experience in academia and in their day-to-day lives. But it became so much bigger than that. It became so much more than my story. It is about the importance of all women speaking freely even when people want to silence us. So that we can become the women our younger selves would be proud of. I hope that people feel compelled to tell their stories and to know that we have nothing to be ashamed of.

I leave you with these questions: Have you ever thought of what would happen if you could talk to a past version of yourself? What year of your life would you talk to? What stories would you tell?

References

Akhurst, J., Solomon, V., Mitchell, C., & Van der Riet, M. (2016). Embedding community-based service learning into psychology degrees at UKZN, South Africa. *Educational Research for Social Change, 5*(2), 136–150. DOI: 10.17159/2221-4070/2016/v5i2a9

Alexander, I. E. (1988). Personality, psychological assessment, and psychobiography. *Journal of Personality, 56*(1), 265–294. DOI: 10.1111/j.1467-6494.1988.tb00469.x

Amosun, S. L., Reddy, P. S., Kambaran, N., & Omardien, R. (2007). Are students in public high schools in South Africa physically active? Outcome of the 1st South African National Youth Risk Behaviour Survey. *Canadian Journal of Public Health, 98*, 254–258. DOI: 10.1007/BF03405398

Bandura, A. (1969). Social-learning theory of identificatory processes. In D. A. Goslin (Ed.), *Handbook of socialization theory and research*. Rand McNally College Publishing.

Bergman, L. R., Cairns, R. B., Nilsson, L.-G., & Nysted, L. (Eds). (2000). *Developmental science and the holistic approach*. Erlbaum.

Bhabha, H. (1994). *The location of culture*. Routledge.

Bickford-Smith, V. (1995). Black ethnicities, communities and political expression in late Victorian Cape Town. *The Journal of African History, 36*(3), 443–465.

Biko, B. S. (1981). I write what I like. *Ufahamu: A Journal of African Studies*, *11*(1). DOI: 10.5070/F7111017260.

Booysen, D. D., & Naidoo, A. V. (2016). On becoming a clinical psychologist: The experiences of initially unsuccessful applicants. *New Voices in Psychology*, *12*(1), 23–39.

Braun, V., & Clarke, V. (2006). Using thematic analysis in psychology. *Qualitative Research in Psychology, 3*(2), 77–101.

Bronfenbrenner, U. (1979). *The ecology of human development: Experiments by nature and design*. Harvard University Press.

Bronfenbrenner, U. (1986). Ecology of the family as a context for human development: Research perspectives. *Developmental Psychology*, *22*(6), 723–742. DOI: 10.1037/0012-1649.22.6.723.

Bronfenbrenner, U. (2005). *Making human beings human: Bioecological perspectives on human development*. Sage.

Bulhan, H. A. (1980). Frantz Fanon: The revolutionary psychiatrist. *Race & Class*, *21*(3), 251–271.

Bulhan, H. A. (2004). *Frantz Fanon and the psychology of oppression*. Springer Science & Business Media.

Cairns, E., & Dawes, A. (1996). Children: Ethnic and political violence – A commentary. *Child Development*, 129–139. DOI: 102.220.210.31.

Cairns, R. B. (1991). Multiple metaphors for a singular idea. *Developmental Psychology, 27*(1), 23-26. DOI: 00I2-1649/9I/S3.00.

Cairns, R. B., & Cairns, B. D. (2006). The making of developmental psychology. In W. Damon & R.M. Lerner (Eds.), *Handbook of child psychology. Vol. 1: Theoretical models of human development* (6th edn, pp. 89–165). Wiley.

Chilisa, B., & Ntseane, G. (2010). Resisting dominant discourses: Implications of indigenous, African feminist theory and methods for gender and education research. *Gender and Education*, *22*(6), 617–632. DOI: 10.1080/09540253.2010.519578

Collins, P. H. (1989). The social construction of black feminist thought. *Signs: Journal of Women in Culture and Society*, *14*(4), 745–773.

Corbera, E., Anguelovski, I., Honey-Rosés, J., &Ruiz-Mallén, I. (2020). Academia in the time of Covid-19: Towards an ethics of care. *Planning Theory & Practice, 21*(2), 191–199.

Curry, C. (1998). Adolescence. In K. Trew & J. Kremer (Eds.), *Gender and psychology.* Oxford University Press.

Doctor, H. V., Mabry, R., Kabudula, C. W., Rashidian, A., Hajjeh, R., Hussain, S. J., & Al-Mandhari, A. (2021). Progress on the health-related Sustainable Development Goals in Eastern Mediterranean Region countries: getting back on track in the time of Covid-19. *Eastern Mediterranean Health Journal, 27*(6), 530–534.

Dhunpath, R. (2000). Life history methodology: "Narradigm" regained. *International Journal of qualitative studies in Education, 13*(5), 543–551.

du Plessis, C. (2017). The method of psychobiography: Presenting a step-wise approach. *Qualitative Research in Psychology, 14*(2), 216–237. DOI: 10.1080/14780887.2017.1284290.

Dwomoh, R. (2021). The conceptualisation of democratic citizenship education by non-Western societies. *Human Rights Education Review, 4*(2), 112–115.

Edmondson, A. (1999). Psychological safety and learning behavior in work teams. *Administrative Science Quarterly, 44*(2), 350–383.

Elms, A. C. (1993). *Uncovering lives: The uneasy alliance of biography and psychology.* Oxford University Press.

Engel, G. L. (1981). The clinical application of the biopsychosocial model. *The Journal of Medicine and Philosophy, 6*(2), 101–124. DOI: 10.1093/jmp/6.2.101

Enslin, P. (2003). Citizenship education in post-apartheid South Africa. *Cambridge Journal of Education, 33*(1), 73–83.

Erikson, E. H. (1950). *Childhood and society.* Penguin.

Erikson, E. H. (1956). The problem of ego identity. *Journal of the American Psychoanalytic Association, 4*, 56–121.

Erikson, E. H. (1958a). The syndrome of identity diffusion in adolescents and young adults. In J. M. Tanner & B. Inhelder (Eds.), *Proceedings of the third meeting of the Child Study Group,*

World Health Organization: Discussions on child development (Vol. 3), (pp. 133–167). International Universities Press.

Erikson, E. H. (1958b). *Young man Luther.* Norton.

Erikson, E. H. (1963). Youth, fidelity and diversity. In E. H. Erikson (Ed.), *Youth, change and challenge* (pp. 1–23). Basic.

Erikson, E. H. (1964). Inner and outer space: Reflections on womanhood. *Daedalus, 93*(2), 582–606.

Erikson, E. H. (1965). Psychoanalysis and ongoing history: Problems of identity, hatred and non-violence. *Journal of the American Psychiatric Association, 122,* 241–250.

Erikson, E. H. (1966). The concept of identity in race relations: Notes and queries. *Daedalus, 95,* 145–170.

Erikson, E. H. (1968). *Identity, youth and crisis.* Norton.

Fanon, F. (1991). *Black skin. White masks.* London

Festa, B. M. (2022). Netflix and the American prison film: Depictions of incarceration and the new prison narrative in Ava DuVernay's 13th (2016). *Hungarian Journal of English and American Studies, 28*(1), 33–43.

Foster, D. E., & Louw-Potgieter, J. E. (1991). *Social psychology in South Africa.* Lexicon Publishers.

Fouche, P., & Van Niekerk, R. (2010). Academic psychobiography in South Africa: Past, present and future. *South African Journal of Psychology, 40*(4), 495–507.

Freud, S. (1964). *Leonardo da Vinci and a memory of his childhood.* Norton.

Gardner, M. M., Aslanzadeh, F. J., Zarrella, G. V., Braun, S. E., Loughan, A. R., & Parsons, M. W. (2021). Cancer, cognition, and Covid: Delivering direct-to-home teleneuropsychology services to neuro-oncology patients. *Neuro-Oncology Practice, 8*(4), 485–496.

Garrett, H. J. (2020). Containing classroom discussions of current social and political issues. *Journal of Curriculum Studies, 52*(3), 337–355.

Gigliotti, R. A., & Fortunato, J. A. (2021). Crisis leadership: A values-centered approach to crisis in higher education. In *A guide for leaders in higher education* (pp. 314–340). Routledge.

Gqola, P. D. (2015). *Rape: A South African nightmare*. Jacana Media.

Gqola, P. D. (2017). *Reflecting rogue: Inside the mind of a feminist*. Melinda Ferguson.

Haine, P., & Booysen, D. D. (2020). Life after training: Professional experiences of early career clinical and counselling psychologists in South Africa. *Journal of Psychology in Africa*, 30(5), 475–483.

Hamand, R. (2020). *White tears/brown scars*. Orion.

Hart, D. M. (1988). Political manipulation of urban space: The razing of District Six, Cape Town. *Urban Geography*, 9(6), 603–628.

Hartsock, N. C. (1997). Comment on Hekman's "Truth and method: Feminist standpoint theory revisited": Truth or justice? *Signs: Journal of Women in Culture and Society*, 22(2), 367–374.

Hedding, D. W., Greve, M., Breetzke, G. D., Nel, W., & Van Vuuren, B. J. (2020). Covid-19 and the academe in South Africa: Not business as usual. *South African Journal of Science, 116*(7-8), 1–3.

Hekman, S. (1997). Truth and method: Feminist standpoint theory revisited. *Signs: Journal of Women in Culture and Society*, 22(2), 341–365.

Hirschmarm, N. J. (1998). Feminist standpoint as postmodern strategy. *Women & Politics*, 18(3), 73–92.

Hook, D. (2001). Critical psychology in South Africa: Applications, limitations, possibilities. *Psychology in Society*, 27, 3–17.

Hook, D. (2012). *A critical psychology of the postcolonial: The mind of apartheid*. Routledge.

Hook, D., Watts, J., & Cockcroft, K. (2002). *Developmental psychology*. Juta.

hooks, b. (1984). Black women: Shaping feminist theory. In *Feminist theory from margin to center* (pp. 1–15). South End Press.

hooks, b. (1991). Theory as liberatory practice. *Yale JL & Feminism*, 4, 1.

Husserl, E. (1983). *Ideas pertaining to a pure phenomenology and to a phenomenological philosophy: First book: General introduction to a pure phenomenology* (Vol. 2). Springer Science & Business Media.

Jacobs, J. A. (2010). Then and now: Activism in Manenberg, 1980 to 2010 [Unpublished master's dissertation]. University of the Western Cape.

Jacobs, L., & Steyn, N. (2013). Commentary: If you drink alcohol, drink sensibly: Is this guideline still appropriate. *Ethnicity & Diseases, 23*(1), 110–115.

Jacobs, L., & Tyree, T. (2013). The construction of femininity, race and sexuality in alcohol advertisements in South African and American women's magazines. *Gender and Behaviour, 11*(2), 5788–5803.

Jansen, J. D. (1990). Curriculum as a political phenomenon: Historical reflections on Black South African Education. *The Journal of Negro Education, 59*(2), 195–206.

Jansen, J. D. (2002). Political symbolism as policy craft: Explaining non-reform in South African education after apartheid. *Journal of Education Policy, 17*(2), 199–215. DOI: 10.1080/02680930110116534

Jansen, J. (2017). *As by fire: The end of the South African university*. Tafelberg.

Jordan, J. (1980). *Passion: New poems, 1977–1980*. Beacon.

Kallaway, P. (2002). *The history of education under apartheid, 1948–1994: The doors of learning and culture shall be opened*. Pearson South Africa.

Kovary, Z. (2011). Psychobiography as a method. The revival of studying lives: New perspectives in personality and creativity research. *Europe's Journal of Psychology, 7*(4), 739–777.

Layne, V. (2008). The District Six Museum: An ordinary people's place. *The Public Historian, 30*(1), 53–62.

Leonard, M. (1998). The long-term unemployed, informal economic activity and the "underclass" in Belfast: Rejecting or reinstating the work ethic. *International Journal of Urban and Regional Research, 22*(1), 42–59.

Lewis, D., & Baderoon, G. (Eds.). (2021). *Surfacing: On being black and feminist in South Africa*. Wits University Press.

Linneberg, M. S., & Korsgaard, S. (2019). Coding qualitative data: A synthesis guiding the novice. *Qualitative Research Journal, 19*(3), 259–270. DOI: 10.1108/QRJ-12-2018-0012

Long, W. (2013). Rethinking "relevance": South African psychology in context. *History of Psychology*, *16*(1), 19. DOI: 10.1037/a0029675.

Lopez-Littleton, V., & Woodley, A. (2018). Movie review of 13th by Ava Duvernay: Administrative evil and the prison industrial complex. *Public Integrity*, *20*(4), 415–418.

Louw, D. A. (1998). *Human development*. (2nd edn.). Kagiso Tertiary.

Maja-Pearce, A. (1994). Left-overs and non-people. *Index on Censorship*, *23*(3), 131–137.

Mandela, M. (1994). *Long walk to freedom*. Abacus.

Manganyi, N. C. (2013). On becoming a psychologist in apartheid South Africa article. *South African Journal of Psychology*, *43*(3), 278–288. DOI: 10.1177/0081246313493

Manganyi, N. C. (2016). *Apartheid and the making of a black psychologist: A memoir*. NYU Press.

Marley, B, & The Wailers. (1980). Redemption song [Song]. On Uprising [Album]. Tuff Gong and Island Records.

Mathabe, N. R. (2018). *The knack of living: The memoir of a psychologist*. Porcupine.

McEachern, C. (1998). Mapping the memories: politics, place and identity in the District Six Museum, Cape Town. *Social Identities*, *4*(3), 499–521.

McGlinchey, E., Hitch, C., Butter, S., McCaughey, L., Berry, E., & Armour, C. (2021). Understanding the lived experiences of healthcare professionals during the Covid-19 pandemic: An interpretative phenomenological analysis. *European Journal of Psychotraumatology*, *12*(1), 1904700.

Mhlanga, D., & Moloi, T. (2021). Covid-19 and Sustainable Development Goals: A comparative analysis of Zimbabwe and South Africa. *African Renaissance*, *18*(1).

Miles, M. B., Huberman, A. M., & Saldaña, J. (2014). *Qualitative data analysis: A methods source-book* (3rd edn). Sage.

Mitchell, G., & Howcroft, G. (2015). Hagiography: Current and prospective contributions. *Journal of Psychology in Africa*, *25*(5), 390–394.

Msimang, S. (2018). *Always another country: A memoir of exile and home*. World Editions.

Mtawa, N., Fongwa, S., & Wilson-Strydom, M. (2021). Enhancing graduate employability attributes and capabilities formation: A service-learning approach. *Teaching in Higher Education, 26*(5), 679–695. DOI: 10.1080/13562517.2019.1672150

New International Version (NIV) Holy Bible. (2009). Biblica.

Nsamenang, A. B., & Dawes, A. (1998). Developmental psychology as political psychology in sub-Saharan Africa: The challenge of Africanisation. *Applied Psychology*, 47(1), 73–87.

Paulse, J. (2019). *Governmentality and disciplinary power: Exploring constitutional values and democratic citizenship education in post-1994 South Africa* [Unpublished doctoral dissertation]. University of the Free State.

Ponterotto, J. G. (2015). Psychobiography in psychology: Past, present, and future. *Journal of Psychology in Africa*, 25(5), 379–389. DOI: 10.1080/14330237.2015.1101267.

Pretorius, L. (2001). *The participation of women in rap music: An exploratory study of the role of gender discrimination* [Unpublished master's dissertation]. University of the Western Cape.

Pretorius, L. J. (2010). *Women's discourses about secretive alcohol dependence and experiences of accessing treatment* [Unpublished doctoral dissertation]. University of Stellenbosch.

Prophets of Da City. (1995). Universal souljaz [Song]. Universal souljaz. Nation Records.

Ramphele, M. (1999). *Across boundaries: The journey of a South African woman leader*. Feminist Press.

Ramrathan, L. (2021). School curriculum in South Africa in the Covid-19 context: An opportunity for education for relevance. *Prospects*, 51(1), 383–392.

Ratele, K., & Duncan, N. (2003). *Social psychology: Identities and relationships*. UCT Press.

Ricoeur, P. (1981). *Hermeneutics and the human sciences: Essays on language, action and interpretation*. Cambridge University Press.

Rosa, E. M., & Tudge, J. (2013). Urie Bronfenbrenner's theory of human development: Its evolution from ecology to bioecology. *Journal of Family Theory & Review, 5*(4), 243–258. DOI: 10.1111/jftr.12022.

Saldaña, J. (2021). *The coding manual for qualitative researchers.* Sage.

Saunders, S. L., & Nedelec, B. (2014). What work means to people with work disability: A scoping review. *Journal of Occupational Rehabilitation, 24,* 100–110.

Schultz, W. T. (Ed.). (2005). *Handbook of psychobiography.* Oxford University Press.

Schultz, W. T., & Lawrence, S. (2017). Psychobiography: Theory and Method. *American Psychologist, 72*(5), 434–445. DOI: 10.1037/amp0000130

Seekings, J. (2000). *The UDF: A history of the United Democratic Front in South Africa, 1983–1991.* New Africa.

Seekings, J. (2008). The continuing salience of race: Discrimination and diversity in South Africa. *Journal of Contemporary African Studies, 26*(1), 1–25.

Skinny_Cow. (2018, December). My virginity. Family Friend Poems. https://www.familyfriendpoems.com/poem/my-virginity

Sneed, J. R., Schwartz, S. J., & Cross, W. E. (2006). A multicultural critique of identity status theory and research: A call for integration. *Identity, 6*(1), 61–84.

Sorell, G. T., & Montgomery, M. J. (2001). Feminist perspectives on Erikson's theory: Their relevance for contemporary identity development research. *Identity: An International Journal of Theory and Research, 1*(2), 97–128.

Stevens, G., & Lockhat, R. (1997). "Coca-Cola Kids": Reflections on black adolescent identity development in post-apartheid South Africa. *South African Journal of Psychology, 27*(4), 250–255.

Suttner, R. (2004). The UDF period and its meaning for contemporary South Africa. *Journal of Southern African Studies, 30*(3), 691–702.

Tabata, I. B. (1960). *Education for barbarism.* Pall Mall.

Timm, J., Block, H., Boanca, G., & Acquaye, H. E. (2022). An exploratory study on the relationship between completion of Erikson's fourth psychosocial stage and assurance of salvation. *Journal of Spirituality in Mental Health*, 24(1), 53–73.

Toquero, C. M. D., & Talidong, K. J. B. (2021). Socio-educational implications of technology use during Covid 19: A case study in General Santos City, Philippines. *Human Behavior and Emerging Technologies*, 3(1), 194–198. DOI: 10.1002/hbe2.214.

Trowler, V. (2018). Book review: Jansen, J. (2017). *As by fire: The end of the South African university*. Pretoria, South Africa: Tafelberg.

Tyree, T. C. M., & Jacobs, L. J. (2014). Can you save me?: Black male superheroes in Hollywood film. *Spectrum: A Journal on Black Men, 3*(1), 1–24.

Van Hal, G., Tavolacci, M. P., Stock, C., Vriesacker, B., Orosova, O., Kalina, O., Salonna, F., Lukacs, A., Ladekjaer Larsen, E., Ladner, J., & Jacobs, L. (2018). European university students' experiences and attitudes toward campus alcohol policy: A qualitative study. *Substance Use & Misuse, 53*(9), 1539–1548. DOI: 10.1080/10826084.2017.1416402

Vygotsky, L. S. (2012). *Thought and language*. MIT Press.

Wegner, L., Stirrup, S., Desai, H., & De Jongh, J. C. (2022). "This pandemic has changed our daily living": Young adults' leisure experiences during the Covid-19 pandemic in South Africa. *Journal of Occupational Science, 29*(3), 323–335.

Wolpe, H. (1995). The uneven transition from apartheid in South Africa. *Transformation, 8*(27), 88–101.

About the author

Professor Liezille J. Jacobs serves as the head of the Department of Psychology at Rhodes University, Makhanda, Eastern Cape, South Africa. Additionally, she held a visiting scholar position at the Department of Psychiatry & Behavioral Science in the School of Medicine at Stanford University. Prof. Jacobs has a doctoral degree in psychology from Stellenbosch University, and was a fellow of the Future Professors Programme (cohort 2, 2021–2023).

Her teaching interests encompass social psychology and critical health psychology, while her research focuses on addiction, the intersections of gender, class, race, identity, and sexuality, feminist epistemologies, and the evolving dynamics of social identities within the realm of cyberpsychology. She also investigates the complex relationship between humans and technology.

Over the past two decades, she has contributed her expertise to organisations such as the South African Medical Research Council (SAMRC), the Human Sciences Research Council (HSRC), the University of the Western Cape (UWC), and has been an Erasmus Mundus Fellow with the Department of Epidemiology and Social Medicines at the University of Antwerpen in Belgium. Her academic journey has also taken her to Howard University in Washington, DC, and she has been actively involved with the South African Monitoring and Evaluation Association (SAMEA).

Prof. Jacobs has an impressive publication record, with over 30 articles published in peer-reviewed international journals. She has also authored multiple book chapters. Notably, she chaired the national Department of Health's alcohol guidelines and served as a committee member of the National Rresearch Foundation (NRF). Her outstanding contributions have earned her awards from the National Institute on Drug Abuse (NIDA) and the Oppenheimer Memorial Trust.

www.ingramcontent.com/pod-product-compliance
Lightning Source LLC
Chambersburg PA
CBHW031136270326
41929CB00011B/1652